TO THE
PRAISE
OF HIS GLORY

—

STUDIES IN EPHESIANS

JOHN W. SMITH

21ST CENTURY CHRISTIAN PUBLISHING

ISBN: 978-0-89098-902-9

©2015 by 21st Century Christian

2809 12th Ave S, Nashville, TN 37204

All rights reserved.

All rights reserved. No part of this publication may be reproduced, stored in a retrieval system, or transmitted in any form or by any means—electronic, mechanical, photocopy, recording, digital, or otherwise—without the written permission of the publisher.

Unless otherwise noted Scripture quotations are from the New American Standard Bible.

Scripture taken from the NEW AMERICAN STANDARD BIBLE®,

Copyright © 1960,1962,1963,1968,1971,1972,1973,1975,1977,1995

by The Lockman Foundation. Used by permission.

Cover design by Jonathan Edelhuber

TABLE OF CONTENTS

Introduction To Ephesians 5

Chapter 1 9

Chapter 2 33

Chapter 3 55

Chapter 4 75

Chapter 5 137

Chapter 6 175

INTRODUCTION TO
EPHESIANS

Many sources will give any interested reader a lengthy, detailed introduction to all the unique and peculiar aspects of Paul's letter to the Church at Ephesus. I do not feel any need to print what others have labored so hard to give us in the area of proof that the Apostle Paul wrote this letter or in all of the idiosyncrasies of this particular city that influenced his writing. In fifty years of preaching and teaching, I have never had anyone express interest or ask questions about who wrote this letter or the subtleties and nuances of the city.

Ephesus was the capital of the Roman province of Asia. In Paul's day, it was the most important city in western Asia Minor (now Turkey). It had a harbor on the Cayster River, which opened on the Aegean Sea. It was famous for trade, art, and culture. It was most famous for the Temple of Diana (Greek, Artemis), which was one of the seven wonders of the ancient world. The temple was 425 ft. long, 240 ft. wide, and had 117 marble columns—60 feet high and six feet in diameter—that supported the roof.

During Paul's time, the governor of Asia lived there. Ephesus had a population between 200,000 and 500,000. The reason for the wide margin of possible residents is that slaves weren't counted as residents, and they probably outnumbered the residents. It was the fourth largest city in the Roman Empire and was a center for occult and mystical speculations. Paul confronted this teaching and caused many to repudiate their connections with magical arts by burning their books with the secret incantations (Acts 19:19). Today the city is in ruins; not a single person lives there.

Paul landed at Ephesus on his second missionary journey, but did not stay (Acts 18:19). He had been forbidden to speak in Asia (Acts 16:6). He went to the synagogue and was received well. He was invited to stay and promised to return. Between that visit and his return, Apollos came and was instructed by Priscilla and Acquila (Acts 18:24). Apparently, he stayed there for several years.

Paul returned in AD 54 (Acts 19) and found some disciples who had been converted by Apollos. A far-reaching and revealing incident takes place when Paul questions these disciples about their baptism and the reception of the Holy Spirit. He began his work, as he usually did, by teaching in the synagogue. After strong opposition from the Jewish leaders, he separated himself from the Jews and began meeting in the school of Tyrannus, where he stayed for three years (Read Acts 19:1-20).

The letter is written from Rome about AD 62 (see Ephesians 6:20) where Paul was a prisoner "in chains" (Ephesians 3:1) and "a prisoner" (4:1). The letter is closely related to Colossians—there are 55 almost identical verses—and both letters were carried by Tychicus (Ephesians 6:22 and Colossians 4:7)—probably on the same trip.

In Acts 20:17, when Paul is on his way to Jerusalem, he stops at Miletus and sends for the elders of the Church at Ephesus. When Paul leaves Ephesus and goes to Macedonia (Acts 19:21), he leaves Timothy in Ephesus. When Paul writes to Timothy the first time and gives him the list of qualifications for elders, Timothy is in Ephesus (1 Timothy 1:3). This is a fascinating sequence because the congregation in Ephesus already had "elders." Acts 14:23 tells us that Paul and Barnabus had "appointed elders" in every city. Although they did not go to Ephesus until the second missionary journey in A.D. 49-52, we have every reason to believe that they continued the practice of appointing elders in every

CHAPTER 1

city. It's noteworthy that they did not appoint elders in every **congregation**, but in every **city**.

Paul comes to Ephesus first in Acts 18:19. He doesn't stay long, but he leaves Priscilla and Aquila there. Soon after he leaves, Apollos comes. Paul returns to Ephesus on the same journey (Acts 19:1) and stayed for two years. He leaves Timothy there and that is where Timothy is when Paul writes his first letter to him. What makes this even more interesting is that he specifically instructs Timothy (1:3) to "**command** certain men not to teach false doctrine." He also instructs him, "**Command** and teach these things" (4:11). Since one part of Timothy's job in Ephesus was to appoint elders, why would he do that if they already had them and why would Paul use the strongest words possible to indicate Timothy's "authority" in Ephesus?

Paul's comments on elders and their appointment also say something about the development of the congregation in Ephesus. By the year 100, Asia Minor was more extensively Christianized than any other land. In his closing remarks in Ephesians 6:21-24, Paul says, "But that you also may know about my circumstances, how I am doing, Tychicus, the beloved brother will tell you everything. and faithful minister in the Lord, will make everything known to you. I have sent him to you for this very purpose, so you may know about us, and that he may comfort your hearts. Peace be to the *brethren*, and love with faith, from God the Father and the Lord Jesus Christ. Grace be with all those who love our Lord Jesus Christ with incorruptible love."

Tychicus is apparently physically carrying this letter to the Ephesian congregations. Paul is relying on him to tell the Ephesian Christians all of the details of his present circumstances. I am interested in Paul's reference to the congregation at Ephesus as "the whole community." It fascinates me that even though Ephesus was a large city, Paul does not write his letter to a particular "congregation" in Ephesus. I am led to wonder if the concept of multiple congregations with multiple leaders in the same city had not yet evolved—or even if that was God's intention?

A discussion of the failure of the Bible translators to translate the Greek word that comes to us as "church" instead of "community," or "called out," or "fellowship," or "congregation" is too long for this study, but the misconceptions created by that failure have led to grossly distorted ideas about the nature of the kingdom of God. Our present system of denominations—each seeking to convert lost people to their "brand" of Christianity—is far from the first-century goal of converting people to Jesus Christ and of Christians only seeing themselves as members of the kingdom of God—not some "branch" of the kingdom and then some particular congregation within that branch. This type of provincial thinking is a gross distortion of what Jesus came to establish.

Ephesus is one of the seven churches of Asia that Jesus addressed through the Apostle John in Revelation—see Revelation 2:10—and it was warned severely by Jesus that if it did not return to its "first love," He would come and "remove its candlestick" from its place (Revelation 2:5). I remind you again, that the city is in ruins, and not a single soul lives there today.

EPHESIANS
CHAPTER 1

¹Paul, an apostle of Christ Jesus by the will of God, to the saints who are at Ephesus, and [who are] faithful in Christ Jesus: ²Grace to you and peace from God our Father and the Lord Jesus Christ. ³Blessed [be] the God and Father of our Lord Jesus Christ, who has blessed us with every spiritual blessing in the heavenly [places] in Christ, ⁴just as He chose us in Him before the foundation of the world, that we would be holy and blameless before Him. In love ⁵He predestined us to adoption as sons through Jesus Christ to Himself, according to the kind intention of His will, ⁶to the praise of the glory of His grace, which He freely bestowed on us in the Beloved. ⁷In Him we have redemption through His blood, the forgiveness of our trespasses, according to the riches of His grace ⁸which He lavished upon us. In all wisdom and insight ⁹He made known to us the mystery of His will, according to His kind intention which He purposed in Him ¹⁰with a view to an administration suitable to the fullness of the times, [that is,] the summing up of all things in Christ, things in the heavens and things on the earth."
(Ephesians 1:1-10)

Paul begins his letter by affirming his apostleship, which he sees as a "providential" intervention—"by the will of God." This point is critical to the thrust of verses 3-14 where the key words are "chose," "predestined," "His pleasure," "mystery," and "purposed."

He then pronounces his customary blessing of grace and peace upon his reading audience. Because it is "customary" does not at all mean that it is trite or superficial. Paul takes it quite seriously and so should we.

Paul uses the phrase "in the heavenly places" five times in this letter and in no other place. Being blessed "in the heavenly places" refers to the place of our citizenship (Philippians 3:20), "But our citizenship is in heaven." It is where Jesus has gone to prepare a place for us and it is where our *treasures* are being laid up. God's blessings are reserved for us "in the heavenly places."

Paul says that all "spiritual" blessings are in Christ. What is a blessing? Blessings are those unlooked for, undeserved, "positive" happenings, outcomes, and circumstances that occur in our daily lives, which we cannot account for, or explain rationally.

What is a spiritual blessing? A spiritual blessing is distinguished from a natural or physical blessing, first by its **source** and second by its "**content.**" Spiritual blessings are the result of God's providential intervention in our lives. They are intended to increase our faith in God's care, as well as our understanding of the purpose and meaning of life, because they affect **who we are**, more than **what we have**.

In 1:4 Paul says, "He *chose* us in Him before the foundation of the world." This passage and others like them have given students of the Word problems for hundreds of years. Even Job struggles with the paradox of "free will" and "predestination." In Job 9, asks, "But how can a man be right before God? Were He to snatch away, who could restrain him? Who could say to Him, 'What are you doing?' "How then can I dispute with him? Though I were innocent, I could not answer him; I could only plead with my Judge for mercy. If it is a matter of strength, he is mighty! And if it is a matter of justice, who will summon him? It is all the same; that is why I say, He destroys both the blameless and the wicked.' If it is not he, then who is it?"

CHAPTER 1

Job asks, "How can I make "free will" decisions when God is all-knowing, all-powerful, and acts arbitrarily?" The Holy Spirit says through Paul that Christians were chosen "to be" something. In this case, they were "chosen to be holy and blameless." We were not simply **destined**; we were destined "for" something. In this case, "destined for adoption as sons," and "destined to be for the praise of his glory" (Ephesians 1:12,14).

In 2 Thessalonians 2:13 Paul writes, "But we should always give thanks to God for you, brethren loved by the Lord, because **God has chosen you** from the beginning for salvation to be saved through the sanctification by the Spirit and faith in the truth." Paul gives further evidence of what God's predestination means. Paul says, "from the beginning," which demonstrates the foreknowledge of God; "God has chosen," but His choosing is not the **individuals** who are going to be saved, but the **methodology** by which they would be saved, which is, "the sanctification of the Spirit" and " faith in the truth."

The rule of thumb that I use for determining the merit of any theory or explanation of the knotty problem of God's predestination and/or foreknowledge is that if it in any way diminishes God's absolute omniscience or denies man's free will, it has no merit. Romans 8:28-30 (also see Romans 9:11-30) sheds even more light on this idea, "And we know that God causes all things to work together for good to *those who love God*, to those who are called according to *His purpose*. For those whom He *foreknew*, He also *predestined* to become conformed to the image of His Son, so that He would be the firstborn among many brethren; and these whom He predestined, He also called; and these whom He called, He also justified; and these whom He justified, He also glorified."

Look at the "qualifying statements" here. God's predestined purpose is, "For those who love God." But loving God is a choice. God "calls" all people to Himself through the gospel, but that call is not irresistible; it demands a response, and responding is a choice. What God predestined is that those who love Him and respond to His call will be conformed to the likeness of Jesus and will be justified.

The inclusiveness of Paul's statement that God *providentially* "works for good in **all** things" troubles us because we can see no good at all in some of the events and circumstances of our lives. Because we cannot **see** any good, it does not mean that there **is** no good. We do not see all ends; in fact, we see quite few. It is also true that the way an infinite mind perceives "good" can be much different from the way a finite mind perceives it. Because God "**works** for good," does not mean that good is always accomplished. God's will is not always done in our lives, and His purposes are not always accomplished in this world.

What does it mean that God "chose" us? It is good to remember that "choosing" does not at all imply that there is no required **response** to the choice. We are not dealing with inanimate objects, like blocks of wood or automobiles. To choose an object is far different from choosing a person. Many a man has "chosen" a bride, only to discover that she has not chosen him. God's choosing demands a response. We must, in turn, "choose Him" to obtain the promise. Our response is voluntary and requires an exercise of the will.

We must also understand what the qualifying phrase "in Him" means. It means that God's choice for man's redemption is *exclusively* bound up in the advent, ministry, death, burial, and resurrection of Jesus. It also means that God has *not chosen* anyone who is outside of Jesus.

What do the collective pronouns "us" and "we" imply? To "choose" means to select from a group, to pick or single out from a number of choices. It implies that we end up with a lesser number than the original. If there is no reduction in numbers, if everything is accepted, no choice has taken place. If I "choose" you, it means that I do *not choose* someone else. The "us" here,

CHAPTER 1

includes the Ephesian Christians and Paul, as well as all others who meet the same criteria. It **excludes** all of those in Ephesus and elsewhere who are not "chosen" and therefore not "in Christ."

God made His choice "before the foundations of the earth." Choosing was part of His eternal plan. We are troubled by these things because they are beyond the comprehension of a finite mind. The question we might frame in this regard might be phrased like this, "If God knew all these things: the fall, the cycle of rejection, rebellion, and the history of sin, why in the name of anything that *makes sense*, did He proceed?" There is no conclusive answer to that, except to say that in His infinite love, wisdom, justice, and mercy, it was the best, wisest, and most loving thing to do.

In Isaiah 55:8-9 God says, "'For My thoughts are not your thoughts, Nor are your ways My ways,' declares the Lord. 'For as the heavens are higher than the earth, So are My ways higher than your ways and My thoughts than your thoughts.'"

Peter, in 2 Peter 3:8-9, sheds some light on this subject when he says, "But do not let this one fact escape your notice, beloved, that with the Lord one day is like a thousand years, and a thousand years like one day. The Lord is not slow about His promise, as some count slowness, but is patient toward you, not wishing for any to perish but for all to come to repentance."

But if God wants everyone to be saved and since salvation is totally at His disposal, why didn't He simply predetermine it? If God had predetermined who is going to be saved and who is going to be lost, there would have been no need for Him to "be patient" to make sure that everyone has a chance to "decide" that they want to be saved.

Ephesians 1:5 tells us that God "predestined us to adoption as sons through Jesus Christ." The implications of the term *predestine* are much more unsettling than the implications of what it means to "choose." It is absolutely critical that we see that this "predestining" was done as a result of His **love**—not arbitrariness or as the result of a whim. No concept of predestination that does not meet the criteria of God's incomprehensible and superintending love is acceptable as an explanation.

To predestine means to deliberately set in motion events and circumstances and to determine beforehand the outcome of those circumstances and events. Something predestined *cannot be changed*. What exactly did God predestine? Paul says that He predetermined "us." In this passage, "us" is a generic, collective pronoun referring to the redeemed. Notice that whatever He predestined for one, He predestined for all. What about the redeemed did God predestine?

1. That they should be holy and blameless ~ "In Christ" vs. 4.
2. That they would be adopted as children. ~ "Through Christ" vs. 5.
3. That their sins would be forgiven ~ "In Him" vs. 7.
4. That the "mystery of His will" would be made known to them ~ "in Christ" vs. 9.
5. That they would receive an inheritance ~ "In Christ" vs. 11.
6. That they would live for the praise of His glory ~ "in Christ" vs. 12.
7. That they would be marked with the seal of the promised Holy Spirit ~ "In Him" vs. 13.

God's decision to redeem man and the methodology for accomplishing that were determined before the foundations of the world. That does not at all mean that He specifically predetermined the **individuals** who would be redeemed; it means that He specifically predetermined the **method** by which they would be redeemed—in Christ.

Notice that all of these "predestined" things are "in Christ."

CHAPTER 1

In Romans 6:23 Paul writes, "For the wages of sin is death, but the free gift of God is eternal life in Christ Jesus our Lord." And in Romans 8:1 he says, "Therefore there is now no condemnation for those who are **in Christ Jesus.**" Second Corinthians 5:17 reads, "Therefore if anyone is in Christ, [he is] a new creature; the old things passed away; behold, new things have come."

What is the significance of **"in Christ"**? How does that take place? Are we "in Christ" by the predestined, arbitrary, and personal selection of God? In Romans 6:3-5 Paul says, "Or do you not know that all of us who have been **baptized** into Christ Jesus have been baptized into His death? Therefore we have been buried with Him through baptism into death, so that as Christ was raised from the dead through the glory of the Father, so we too might walk in newness of life. For if we have become **united with Him** in the likeness of His death, certainly we shall also be **in the likeness of His** resurrection."

The only way that we can be "in Christ" is to be born from above in baptism. Although immersion in the water of baptism is a **predestined condition** of being "in Christ," the decision to meet that condition is a **choice**. In Colossians 2:8-12 Paul warns the Christians at Colossi, "See to it that no one takes you captive through philosophy and empty deception, according to the tradition of men, according to the elementary principles of the world, rather than according to Christ. For **in Him** all the fullness of Deity dwells in bodily form, and you in Him have been made complete, and He is the head over all rule and authority; **And in Him** you were also circumcised with a circumcision made without hands, in the removal of the body of the flesh by the circumcision of Christ, having been **buried with Him in baptism**, in which you were also raised up with Him through faith in the working of God, who raised Him from the dead."

"See to it," means that **we** have something to do with the results. "Through faith" places the responsibility on us for all of God's work. "If" anyone is in Christ, implies that there are those who are not. Why are they not? The Hebrew writer, in 4:6 says, "Therefore, since it remains for some to enter it, and those who formerly had good news preached to them failed to enter because of disobedience."

The choosing and the destining are generic. God has not chosen individuals, but a **group**, and His choosing is based not on His arbitrary whim, but on our choosing Him. **Free will and predestination are not mutually exclusive**. It is entirely probable that God not only has, but that He continues to "predestine" certain events and people for His glory. Paul's troublesome analogy about the potter and the clay in Romans 9:15-21, cannot be understood otherwise, "For he says to Moses, 'I will have mercy on whom I have mercy, and I will have compassion on whom I have compassion.' So then it does not depend on the man who wills or the man who runs, but on God who has mercy. For the Scripture says to Pharaoh, 'For this very purpose I raised you up, to demonstrate My power in you, and that My name might be proclaimed throughout the whole earth.' **So then He has mercy on whom He desires, and He hardens whom He desires**. You will say to me then, 'Why does He still find fault? For who resists His will?' On the contrary, who are you, O man, who answers back to God? The thing molded will not say to the molder, 'Why did you make me like this?' Or does not the potter have a right over the clay, to make from the same lump one vessel for honorable use and another for common use?"

One basic principle about the nature of God must be constantly applied. God cannot be boxed in by arbitrary parameters of our choosing. He cannot be confined by our sense of justice, fair play, consistency, or logic. We ought to learn that from Job.

All of God's grace is summed up in a single word—*Jesus*. There are many applications, but all of them have the same source. In the NIV, Ephesians 1:6 tells us that grace was "lavished"

CHAPTER 1

on us. *Lavished* is a term that suggests abundance beyond need or desire, but it was lavished within the confines of God's wisdom, justice, and plan. It is easy to forget that it is God's grace, and His grace is restricted to His conditions for meting it out and those conditions are "in Christ." All salvation options are restricted to a single possibility: "There is no other name under heaven that has been given among men by which we must be saved" (Acts 4:12). That is the way that God set it up, and it is irrevocable and unchangeable.

"He made known to us the mystery" (Ephesians 1:9). Paul explains the "mystery" in Ephesians 3:6, when he says that the **mystery** is that through the gospel of the cross, the Gentiles have become heirs of the promise made to Abraham that in his **seed**, (Jesus) **all nations** will be blessed and together, will become the new Israel of God, where all members form one body and share together in that promise.

All of the purposes God had for mankind when He created them did not end when Adam and Eve sinned; they were only postponed. The sin of Adam and Eve initiated the unfolding of God's eternal plan for not only their redemption, but the redemption of all of their posterity who likewise would fall under the power of sin. Consequently, we witness the introduction of the sacrificial altar; the Mosaic instructions and prohibitions; the prophetical promises and enlightenment; the coming of the Christ; His ministry and death, burial, and resurrection. All of that pointed to the Pentecostal proclamation of the gospel, which allowed Jew and Gentile to "share" in the promise made to Abraham that **all nations** would be blessed.

In 3:5 we learn that this mystery was revealed exclusively to the prophets and apostles in the Christian era. In 3:8-9 we learn that it became Paul's responsibility to make the mystery plain by explaining it and by administering it—actually putting it into practice. In 3:11 we learn that this revealing and administering fulfilled God's eternal purpose, which He accomplished through Christ.

In 1 Corinthians 13 Paul tells us that, "We see in a mirror dimly." That helps us to understand **why** God's choice to redeem mankind in this way still **remains a mystery**. The complete revelation of this mystery will happen when this mortal puts on immortality, when we are changed—clothed with the imperishable and we shall know fully as our "finiteness" is swallowed up in God.

"He made known to us the mystery of His will, according to His kind intention, which He purposed in Him, with a view to an administration suitable to the fullness of the times, that is, the summing up of all things in Christ, things in the heavens and things on the earth" (Ephesians 1:9-10).

Paul says that God has revealed the final step in His plan to redeem mankind. He revealed it when He decided it was time to do so, and He revealed it according to His plan. His "purpose" was always to send Jesus to redeem us. The "time of fulfillment" is simply the time that God decided to bring His plan to fruition. God's plan was to place the redemption of all creation in the hands of the Christ.

Questions Over Ephesians 1:1-10

1. What is the "heavenly realm?"
2. What is a *spiritual* blessing?
3. How can we make "free will" decisions when God is all-knowing, all-powerful and acts arbitrarily?
4. What does it mean to predetermine (predestine) something?
5. What exactly did God predestine?
6. Do you believe that certain things in your life were predetermined?

CHAPTER 1

7. If God wants everyone to be saved and since salvation is totally at His disposal, why didn't He simply predetermine it?
8. How does a person get "in Christ" and what is the significance of that?
9. What did God predestine about those who are "in Christ?"
10. All of God's grace is summed up in what one word?

¹¹"In Him also we have obtained an inheritance, having been predestined according to His purpose who works all things after the counsel of His will, ¹² to the end that we who were the first to hope in Christ should be to the praise of His glory. ¹³ In Him, you also, after listening to the message of truth, the gospel of your salvation—having also believed, you were sealed in Him with the Holy Spirit of promise, ¹⁴ who is given as a pledge of our inheritance, with a view to the redemption of [God's own] possession, to the praise of His glory."
(Ephesians 1:11-14)

God *predestined*—He **chose** to redeem, save, adopt, accept as His children those human beings who **choose** to accept the sacrifice of His Son, Jesus Christ. He did that, because **it pleased Him** to do it. He did it because of His love for us. He also did it because it magnified His grace. We see an interesting side of God's personality revealed in His decision to do things simply because it pleases Him to do it. God created a universe and everything in it and He created mankind, simply because it pleased Him. We also see a side of our own personality—created in the image of God—because we often do things simply because it pleases us to do them.

"We who were the first" (Ephesians 1:12). The "We" may be in deference to the "you also" of verse 13. If so, it means that the apostles and Paul were the first to hear and accept the gospel. The purpose of our life in Jesus is to bring praise to God.

The Christians in Ephesus all heard and received the *same* gospel, they inherited the *same* hope, and they also received the *same* gift of the Holy Spirit. They were "included" (in the body of Christ) when they "heard the word of truth"—the "gospel of salvation"—and "believed" (Ephesians 1:13).

Both hearing and believing are active in this case. We need to remember that Jesus talked extensively about those who hear and do not *understand*, and James makes specific reference to those who believe but do not *act*. Once again we are reminded that God's predestination and choosing do not preclude the necessity of hearing and believing, both of which are matters of choice.

Paul says that God "marked" them (the Christians in Ephesus) with the Holy Spirit. That means that God **distinguished** those who are "born from above" from all others by declaring ownership. The Holy Spirit is a "seal"—a personal guarantee—a certification, verification, that God has kept His promises to us. Those promises are that He will forgive, redeem, declare righteous, save and sanctify those who obey the gospel. The perennial question, "How do I *know* I'm saved?" is answered first *objectively*, through our obedience to God's commands to repent, confess, and physically comply with the call of the gospel in baptism; it is also answered *subjectively*, through the indwelling Holy Spirit who leads, intercedes, convicts, brings joy, patience, hope, and guides us into truth.

The Holy Spirit is given to fulfill God's long-standing promise: "This is that which was spoken of by **the prophet Joel**, 'I will pour forth of my Spirit on all mankind" (Acts 2:16-17); "On the last day, the great day of the feast, Jesus stood and cried out saying, 'If anyone is thirsty, let him come to Me and drink. He who believes in Me, **as the Scripture said**, "From his innermost being will flow rivers of living water."' By this He spoke of the Spirit, whom *those who believed* in him were to receive; for the Spirit was not yet given, because Jesus was not yet glorified" (John 7:37-39).

CHAPTER 1

Notice the critical importance of the prerequisite of faith to receive the Holy Spirit. In Ephesians 1:13 Paul says, "**having also believed**," you were marked with the Holy Spirit. In Galatians 3:1-5 Paul asks the Christians at Galatia, "Did you receive the Spirit by the works of the Law, or by hearing with faith? ...Does He who provides you with the Spirit and works miracles among you, do it by the works of the Law, or by hearing with faith?"

In 2 Thessalonians 2:13 Paul writes, "But we should always give thanks to God for you, brethren beloved by the Lord, because God has chosen you from the beginning for salvation through the sanctification by the Spirit and faith in the truth." Paul says that the sanctifying work of the Holy Spirit is a **prerequisite** to salvation. It is just as important as faith, penitence, confession, and baptism. If we really believe that, it seems to me that we ought to be talking about it and emphasizing it more.

What is the "sanctifying work" of the Holy Spirit? The most commonly accepted definition of sanctification is a good one: "set apart." But what does it mean to be "set apart?" Set apart for what—to what? Notice that we do not sanctify ourselves. Sanctification is the work of the Holy Spirit, and we may thank God for that, because if it was left up to us it would never get done.

The sanctifying work of the Holy Spirit causes us to be "set apart to"—totally focused on Jesus. A good illustration of this is in John 15:1-8 where Jesus gives the analogy of the vine and the branches. Please pay attention to the fact that the **focus** is on the **vine**, not the **branches**. The reason why the Holy Spirit is sanctifying us—setting us apart to Jesus—is because Jesus said—"**Apart from Me** you can do **nothing**" (John 15:5).

Jesus said, "Go into all the world and preach the gospel to all creation" (Mark 16:15). Our response has traditionally been to focus on the *needs* of the people to whom we are going to preach rather than *the command of Jesus*. Our motivation for preaching to the lost is **not** because they have needs; our motivation is the command of Jesus. We often set about doing "Christian" works by having brainstorming planning sessions in which we try to figure out what the best marketing strategy to a successful venture would be. We often forget that unless we are totally focused on—completely set apart to—and completely sanctified to Jesus, we can do **nothing**!

Remember that the work of the Holy Spirit is to bring glory to Jesus—not to Himself. John says in 16:13-14, "But when he, the Spirit of truth, comes, He will guide you into all truth; for He will not speak on his own initiative, but whatever He hears, He will speak; and He will disclose to you what is to come. **He will glorify Me**, for He will take of mine and will disclose it to you."

The Spirit is given to us by God to **assure us** of His presence and His promise. Second Corinthians 5:3-5 teaches, "For indeed while we are in this tent, we groan, being burdened, because we do not want to be unclothed but to be clothed, so that what is mortal will be swallowed up by life. Now He who prepared us for this very purpose is God, who gave to us the Spirit as a pledge."

How does the Spirit guarantee us that we are in a right relationship with God?

1. By His **fruits**: "But the *fruit of the Spirit* is love, joy, peace, patience, kindness, goodness, faithfulness, gentleness, self-control; against such things there is no law. Now those who belong to Christ Jesus have crucified the flesh with its passions and desires. If we live by the Spirit, let us also walk by the Spirit. Let us not become boastful, challenging one another, envying one another" (Galatians 5:22-26).

    Let us never forget that these "fruits" are the work of the Holy Spirit, not qualities that "we" produce through our own determination and self discipline. The presence of these fruits in our lives, assures us of our relationship with God because without the indwelling Spirit, they would not be there.

CHAPTER 1

2. By our **prayers**: "In the same way the Spirit also helps our weakness; for we do not know how to pray as we should, but the Spirit Himself intercedes for *us* with groanings too deep for words; and He who searches the hearts knows what the mind of the Spirit is, because He intercedes for the saints according to *the will of* God" (Romans 8:26-27).

    If we can see or feel a "presence" or an "influence" in our prayer life that is obviously outside of ourselves, we are assured of the Spirit's sanctifying work in us.

3. By His **testimony**: "For you have not received a spirit of slavery leading to fear again, but you have received a spirit of adoption as sons by which we cry out, 'Abba! Father!'" (Romans 8:15-16).

    The Spirit himself *testifies* with our spirit that we are God's children. The Holy Spirit "communicates" with that "spirit" that He created in us when we were "born from above," bringing assurance of God's providential care, guidance, conviction and intervention.

4. By the power to **overcome sin**: "So then, brethren, we are under obligation, not to the flesh, to live according to the flesh—for if you are living according to the flesh, you must die; but if by the Spirit you are putting to death the deeds of the body, you will live" (Romans 8:12-13).

    If sin is dominating our lives, we can be assured that we are not utilizing the Holy Spirit power available to us to conquer it.

5. Because of His **leading**: "For all who are being led by the Spirit of God, these are sons of God" (Romans 8:14).

    This assurance is especially important in our decision-making processes. We need to be confident that the indwelling Spirit is seeking to influence our decision making when we are open to His leading.

6. Because **God's love is in our hearts** through the indwelling Spirit: "And hope does not disappoint because the love of God has been poured out within our hearts through the Holy Spirit who was given to us" (Romans 5:5).

    What a precious thought! We can learn to love as God does, because the Holy Spirit is constantly "pouring" into our hearts a love that allows us to love others, not from a worldly, human point-of-view, but from an otherworldly, spiritual point-of-view.

7. By **the scriptures**, which contain the promises of God: The Holy Spirit increases our understanding of the Bible and brings it to life in the believer (1 Corinthians 2:12).

8. By His **convicting work**: Jesus says in John 16:8 that when the Holy Spirit comes He will convict the world of sin, righteousness, and judgment. If we are not under conviction in these areas, it is a good sign that the Holy Spirit is not at work in us.

This takes us back to God's purpose in saving us. Read Ephesians 1:1-14 again: "*That* we might be *holy and blameless* before Him in love." vs. 6 "to the praise of his glorious grace;" vs. 12 "that we might live for the praise of His glory." Sin cannot stand in the presence of God. The only way we can be in fellowship with Him is to be "holy"—sinless—and the only way we can be sinless is for God to make us so. All of this—the eight points above—is accomplished through the indwelling Spirit. If we walk around unsure of our salvation, guilt-ridden, sin-laden, selfish, materialistic, complaining, whining, unconvicted, unforgiving, cynical, and fearful, there is no praise to His glorious grace.

Questions Over Ephesians 1:11-14

1. All of God's grace is summed up in what words?

CHAPTER 1

2. What does it mean that God "marked" them with the Holy Spirit?
3. How is the perennial question, "How do I *know* I'm saved?" answered?
4. Second Thessalonians 2:13 tells us that our salvation depends on the "sanctifying work of the Holy Spirit." What is the "sanctifying work" of the Holy Spirit?
5. If we accept the common definition of sanctification as "set apart," what does that mean? Set apart for what—to what?
6. How does the Holy Spirit "set us apart?"
7. Why do you suppose that we don't talk about this more?
8. The Spirit is given to us to **assure us** of God's presence and His promise. How does He do that?
9. In 2 Corinthians 3:2-5, Paul says that the Holy Spirit *guarantees* "what is to come." How does the Spirit do that?
10. Name eight ways the Spirit guarantees us that we are in a right relationship with God?

[15] "For this reason I too, having heard of the faith in the Lord Jesus which [exists] among you, and your love for all the saints, [16] do not cease giving thanks for you, while making mention [of you] in my prayers; [17] that the God of our Lord Jesus Christ, the Father of glory, may give to you a spirit of wisdom and of revelation in the knowledge of Him. [18] [I pray that] the eyes of your heart may be enlightened, so that you may know what is the hope of His calling, what are the riches of the glory of His inheritance in the saints, [19] and what is the surpassing greatness of His power toward us who believe. [These are] in accordance with the working of the strength of His might [20] which He brought about in Christ, when He raised Him from the dead and seated Him at His right hand in the heavenly [places,] [21] far above all rule and authority and power and dominion, and every name that is named, not

only in this age, but also in the one to come. ²²And He put all things in subjection under His feet, and gave Him as head over all things to the church, ²³ which is His body, the fullness of Him who fills all in all."
(Ephesians 1:15-23)

When Paul wrote, "For this reason," He wanted them to know how grateful he was that they were allowing God to do His work in them. He also wanted them to know that he prayed for them and what he prayed for. We all find it encouraging knowing that people are praying for us.

Paul's prayer is that God will give them "the spirit of wisdom, and revelation" (v.17). What is "the spirit of wisdom?" Please pay careful attention to the word, *"the* spirit"—not "a spirit." If we ask how Paul expects God to answer his prayer, we need to look in Ephesians 3:16-17. The answer is that these internal, spiritual qualities are given through the indwelling Holy Spirit.

The question of "how" God answers our prayers is an interesting and important question because it impacts not only what we pray for, but how much faith we have in God's answers. If we pray for something but have no idea how God could possibly respond, it weakens our fervency and confidence. For instance, if I have a bad temper and I pray that God will help me to overcome it, but I can see absolutely no way for Him to do that, I can have little confidence in His response to my prayer? I know that He isn't going to perform a frontal lobotomy or turn a screw. God answers all of our prayers for internal or spiritual needs like being more patient, loving, bold, kind, generous or forgiving through the agency of the indwelling Holy Spirit.

If we then ask, "How does the Holy Spirit help us to accomplish things like I just mentioned?" The answer is that He accomplishes that through *communication* with the "Spirit" that He made to dwell in us when we were born from above in baptism.

The "spirit of wisdom" that Paul talks about is not wisdom

CHAPTER 1

in the educational, experiential, and material sense. It is wisdom in the "spiritual, supernatural" sense. Paul speaks of a wisdom that does not come through worldly, material, educational, and environmental processes. If spiritual wisdom could be gained that way, the more intellectually gifted would have an advantage over those less gifted. In 1 Corinthians 2:6-8, Paul specifically states that the wisdom he speaks of is, "a wisdom not of this age nor of the rulers of this age, who are passing away; but we speak God's wisdom in a mystery, the hidden wisdom which God predestined before the ages to our glory; the wisdom which none of the rulers of this age has understood; for if they had understood it, they would not have crucified the Lord of glory."

Again from 1 Corinthians 12:7-8, "But to each one is given the manifestation of the Spirit for the common good. For one is given the word of wisdom through the Spirit, and to another the word of knowledge according to the same Spirit." Paul's emphasis is not so much on the gifts, which are different, but on the gift giver—who is the same. Pay close attention to the fact that it is not wisdom and revelation we receive. What we receive is the spirit of wisdom and revelation. There is a **big** difference! Spiritual wisdom and discernment come through the indwelling Holy Spirit.

Please take the time to read slowly and carefully this passage from 1 Corinthians 2:1-13 in which Paul says, ""And when I came to you, brethren, I did not come with superiority of speech or of wisdom, proclaiming to you the testimony of God. For I determined to know nothing among you except Jesus Christ, and Him crucified. And I was with you in weakness and in fear and in much trembling, and my message and my preaching were not in persuasive words of wisdom, but in demonstration of the Spirit and of power, so that your faith would not rest on the wisdom of men, but on the power of God. Yet we do speak wisdom among those who are mature; a wisdom, however, not of this age, nor of the rulers of this age, who are passing away; but we speak God's wisdom in a mystery, the hidden [wisdom,] which God predestined before the ages to our glory; [the wisdom] which none of the rulers of this age has understood; for if they had understood it, they would not have crucified the Lord of glory; For to us God revealed [them] **through the Spirit**; for the Spirit searches all things, even the depths of God. For who among men knows the [thoughts] of a man except the spirit of the man, which is in him? Even so the [thoughts] of God no one knows except **the Spirit of God**. Now **we have received**, not the spirit of the world, but **the Spirit who is from God, that** we might know the things freely given to us by God, which things we also speak, not in words taught by human wisdom, but in those **taught by the Spirit**, combining spiritual [thoughts] with spiritual [words.]."

What an incredible passage with a fantastic message for us! We seldom appreciate the uniqueness of who we are in Christ and the wisdom, the peace, the perspective on life that we possess because of the Spirit's indwelling! That is why Paul writes in Colossians 3:16, "Let the word of Christ richly dwell within you, with all wisdom teaching and admonishing one another with psalms and hymns and spiritual songs, singing with thankfulness in your hearts to God."

Now, what is this "Spirit of revelation" and why do we need it? To *reveal* means to make known, to take the cover off. We can get some insight into the purpose of the "Spirit of revelation" by looking at what the gift is supposed to accomplish. In Ephesians 3:2-3 Paul writes, "Indeed you have heard of the stewardship of God's grace which was given to me for you; that by revelation there was made known to me the mystery, as I wrote before in brief." In Romans 16:25-26 he says, "Now to him who is able to establish you in accordance with my gospel, the message I proclaim about Jesus Christ, in keeping with the *revelation* of the mystery hidden for long ages past, but *now revealed* and made

CHAPTER 1

known through the prophetic writings by the command of the eternal God, so that all the Gentiles might come to the obedience that comes from faith" (NIV).

Paul says that he is praying that God will give them the Spirit of Revelation "so that." Always pay close attention to the **"so that's."**

1. The Spirit of revelation is given **"so that"** they may know God better. We can see the incredible importance of that when we read John 17:3 where Jesus says, "Now this is eternal life: that they **know you**, the only true God, and Jesus Christ, whom you have sent" (NIV). Jesus says that "knowing God" is equivalent to salvation. In 2 Thessalonians 1:7-8 Paul writes, "This will happen when the Lord Jesus is revealed from heaven in blazing fire with his powerful angels. He will **punish those** who **do not know God** and do not obey the gospel of our Lord Jesus" (NIV).

2. **So that** the "eyes of our hearts might be enlightened." Jeremiah 31:33, "But this is the covenant which I will make with the house of Israel after those days," declares the LORD, "I will put My law within them, and **on their heart I will write it**; and I will be their God, and they shall be My people."

    When the eyes of the heart are enlightened, we will understand the nature of the God's new covenant—that it differs from the Old Covenant in that it contains divine spiritual principles applicable to every conceivable situation of life—not divine commandments to be interpreted and applied legalistically.

3. **So that** we might *know* the hope in Jesus. *Know* in this case, means that we can actually experience and feel the hope we have in Jesus—not just be intellectually aware of it.

4. **So that** we might *know*, (experience) "the riches of His inheritance."

5. **So that** we might *know* (experience) "His great power"—the power to redeem us; power to forgive us; power to encourage us; power to sanctify and transform us and power to free us from the tyranny of self interest.

   Paul expands on that power, describing it as the power that raised Jesus from the dead. In Ephesians 1:20, it is the power that elevated Jesus to His position as High Priest. In Hebrews 8:1 it is the power that placed all things in subjection to Him, including Satan and death. It is the power that made Him head of the Church, which is His fullness—the complete representation of Jesus on the earth.

The overall purpose of these gifts is to know (experience) God's incomparably great power, which is like the working of His mighty strength. Why were the disciples to stay in Jerusalem? It was so they could receive power. And that power came in the form of the Holy Spirit.

Jesus is *head* over all things for The Church. The Church is *subject* to Jesus in all things. The Church is the body of Jesus; the body is the fullness of Jesus; and Jesus fills everything.

Questions Over Ephesians 1:15-23

1. How does Paul expect God to answer his prayer that He will give the Christians at Ephesus the "Spirit of wisdom?" What is "he Spirit of wisdom?"
2. What is the "Spirit of revelation"? To reveal means to make known. What is the Spirit going to make known?
3. Paul prays that God will give them the Spirit of Revelation "so that." What are the "so that's?"

CHAPTER 1

4. Why is it so important that they know God better?
5. How does God answer all of our prayers for internal or spiritual needs?
6. How does the Holy Spirit help us to accomplish things like being more patient, loving, bold, kind, generous, or forgiving through the agency of the indwelling Holy Spirit?
7. What is the difference between receiving wisdom and revelation and receiving the *Spirit* of wisdom and revelation?
8. What is the purpose of these gifts of wisdom and revelation?

EPHESIANS
CHAPTER 2

¹"And you were dead in your trespasses and sins, ² in which you formerly walked according to the course of this world, according to the prince of the power of the air, of the spirit that is now working in the sons of disobedience. ³Among them we too all formerly lived in the lusts of our flesh, indulging the desires of the flesh and of the mind, and were by nature children of wrath, even as the rest. ⁴But God, being rich in mercy, because of His great love with which He loved us, ⁵even when we were dead in our transgressions, made us alive together with Christ (by grace you have been saved), ⁶and raised us up with Him, and seated us with Him in the heavenly [places,] in Christ Jesus, ⁷so that in the ages to come He might show the surpassing riches of His grace in kindness toward us in Christ Jesus. ⁸For by grace you have been saved through faith; and that not of yourselves, [it is] the gift of God; ⁹not as a result of works, that no one may boast. ¹⁰For we are His workmanship, created in Christ Jesus for good works, which God prepared beforehand, that we should walk in them."
(Ephesians 2:1-10)

Paul reminds the Christians in Ephesus that there was a time when they were "dead." He tells them that their death was caused by transgressions and sins. In Romans 7:8-11, Paul expands on this theme of death caused by transgressions and sins when he says, "But sin, taking opportunity through the commandment, produced in me coveting of every kind; for apart from the Law sin [is] dead. And **I was once alive** apart from the Law; but when the commandment came, sin became alive, and **I died**; and this commandment, which was to result in life, proved to result in death for me; for **sin**, taking an opportunity through the commandment, deceived me, and through it **killed me**."

The kind of death caused by sins is obviously not physical, which leaves only one other possibility. In Christian terms, it is called *spiritual death*. Notice the following passages:

- 1 Timothy 5:6: "But the widow who lives for pleasure is **dead** even **while she lives**" (NIV). Paul says that in God's sight, death is not defined as the cessation of physical life; it is defined by our relationship to Him.

- Ephesians 5:13-14: "But all things become visible when they are exposed by the light, for everything that becomes visible is light. For this reason it says, "Awake, sleeper, and **arise from the dead**, and Christ will shine on you." Paul exhorts those who are disobedient—consequently sin dominated—to rise from the dead. The death from which they are encouraged to rise can be nothing but **spiritual death.**

- Romans 8:6: "For the mind set on the flesh is death, but the mind set on the Sprit is life and peace." Paul says that the *mind* of sinful man is *death*. What kind of "mind" leads to death? The answer is—a mind controlled by sin. To what *kind* of death does a mind controlled by sin lead? It has to be "**spiritual** death" since these people are still physically alive.

In Ephesians 2:1, Paul says that the Christians in Ephesus used to **live** in transgressions and sins. Most of us have heard the term "living in sin" applied to a person who continues to commit the same sin over and over again. According to Paul's

CHAPTER 2

words, "living in sin" refers to "following the ways of this world." So what exactly does "following the ways of this world" look like in practical terms?

We normally think of sin as something we "commit." If we tell a lie or steal $10.00, we "commit" a sin. When we say that, we mean that we are guilty of a single, vertical, and specific sinful action. "Living in sin" has to do with a horizontal *state of being*—a condition of life.

What Paul states in the passage above is that "living in sin" is following the world's desires and thoughts. "Living in sin" is a *condition of life* that has to do with our **core value** structure, which is the mental process by which we make decisions. "Living in sin" is essentially the difference between "**telling** a lie"—and "**being** a liar." Telling a lie makes a person a sinner—but it does not necessarily make them "a liar." A liar is a person who lies incessantly—whose life is dominated by lies. Paul says that "living in sin" is spiritual death.

(* *Please see notes on core values on page 52.*)

Look closely at this poignant passage from Romans 6 where Paul asks, "How shall we who **died to sin** still **live in it**? Or do you not know that all of us who have been **baptized into Christ** Jesus have been **baptized into His death**? Therefore we have been **buried with Him** through baptism into death, in order that as Christ was raised from the dead through the glory of the Father, so we too might walk in **newness of life**. For if we have become united with [Him] in the likeness of His death, certainly we shall be also [in the likeness] of His resurrection, knowing this, that **our old self** was crucified with [Him,] in order that our **body of sin** might be done away with, so that we would no longer be **slaves** to sin" (2-6).

Paul is saying that it is **impossible** for a person who has been born from above in a baptism into the death of Jesus to still live in sin. He does not say, nor does he mean that a person cannot "commit sin," he says that they can no longer live in the condition of sin because the "body of sin"—the body controlled by fleshly desires—has been done away with.

Paul says (vs. 3) that those who live in sin are **by nature** objects of wrath. The "nature" to which Paul refers is the "divine nature" that cannot tolerate sin. Romans 8:5-9 presents us with a startling contrast between **living** according to the sinful (fleshly) nature and **living** according to the Spirit-led nature. "Those who **live** (have a lifestyle in harmony with) according to the flesh have their *minds* set on what **the** flesh desires; but those who **live** (have a lifestyle in harmony) in accordance with the Spirit have their **minds set** on what the Spirit desires. The *mind* (decision making process) governed by the flesh is ***death***, but the *mind* (decision making process) governed by the Spirit is **life** and peace. The *mind* governed by the flesh (the mind controlled by material, fleshly desires) is hostile to God; *it does not submit* to God's law, nor **can it do so**. Those **who are in the realm of the flesh** cannot please God. You, (Those who have been born from above) however, are not in the realm of the flesh but are in the realm of the Spirit, if indeed the Spirit of God lives in you. And if anyone does not have the Spirit of Christ, they do not belong to Christ" (NIV).

Notice that the spiritual death of the Christians in Ephesus was caused (vs.1) by following "the ways of this world and of the ruler of the kingdom of the air, the spirit who is now at work in those who are disobedient." Who is the "spirit now at work?" It is the antithesis of the Holy Spirit who is also "now at work." What this means is that there are two opposing forces at work in our lives—God and Satan. God is trying to draw us closer to Him, and Satan is trying to draw us closer to him. That is why Paul warns us in Ephesians 6:10-12 **who** our "struggle" is against.

Notice that Paul speaks of being lost or saved as the result of what we have our "minds" set on—and what we set our minds on is a decision. **We decide** what we read, watch, listen to and talk about and those decisions are directly responsible for what

CHAPTER 2

our minds are set on. If we read, watch, listen to and talk about things that are spiritually uplifting and convicting, the Holy Spirit can control our thinking and decision making. If we read, watch, listen to, and talk about what is worldly and materialistic, Satan controls our thinking and decision making.

To be spiritually dead means that **we** have no strength, no power to overcome fleshly desires or to accomplish the noble thoughts and higher aspirations that occasionally arise within us. Every person occasionally has a desire to be better; to be kinder, more patient, more loving, and more selfless, but often those noble thoughts are drowned out by self-centered, materialistic voices, and the result is that sin has dominion over our higher thoughts.

I suspect that few, if any sins are committed out of ignorance. We know what we are about to do is wrong; we may even hate ourselves for doing it, but still we come up with some rationale or justification and proceed because we lack the moral power to say *no* to ourselves. As Paul wrote in Romans 7:19, "For the good that I want, I do not do, but I practice the very evil that I do not want."

In extreme cases, people become animalistic, torturing, abusing, even killing their own children and justifying things like pornography, abortion, torture, homosexuality, and euthanasia. In Romans 1:25-28 Paul describes the extreme evil that people are capable of when God is removed from their minds. "For they exchanged the truth of God for a lie, and **worshiped and served the creature** rather than the Creator, who is blessed forever. Amen. For this reason **God gave them over** to degrading passions; for their women exchanged the natural function for that which is unnatural, and in the same way also the men abandoned the natural function of the woman and burned in their desire toward one another, men with men committing indecent acts and receiving in their own persons the due penalty of their error. And just as they did not see fit to acknowledge God any longer,

God gave them over to a depraved mind, to do those things which are not proper."

In Ephesians 2:3 Paul makes a sweeping statement by saying that everybody—yes, even you and I—are either presently—or have been in the past—spiritually dead. He goes on to say that as a result of that death, we were, "children of wrath." What does it mean to be a "child of wrath?"

Spiritual death is the "natural state" of unregenerate man. In Romans 1:18; Paul says that all who are in that dead state are objects of wrath—things that **God is going to destroy.**

In 2 Thessalonians 1:6-10 Paul writes, "God is just: **He will pay back** trouble to those who trouble you and give relief to you who are troubled, and to us as well. This will happen when the Lord Jesus is revealed from heaven in blazing fire with his powerful angels. He will **punish those** who **do not know God** and do not obey the gospel of our Lord Jesus. *They will be punished with* **everlasting destruction** and shut out from the presence of the Lord and from the majesty of his power on the day he comes to be glorified in his holy people and to be marveled at among all those who have believed. **This includes you**, because you believed our testimony to you" (NIV).

Matthew says of Jesus in Matthew 3:12, "His winnowing fork is in his hand, and he will clear his threshing floor, gathering his wheat into the barn and burning up the chaff with unquenchable fire" (NIV).

Ephesians 2:3 makes it obvious that the Christians in Ephesus are no longer spiritually dead and are no longer objects of wrath. The question is how and when did this change take place? In 2:4 Paul says, "**but**"—probably the most important "**but**" in the Bible, "but because of His great love for us **God made us alive.**" What prompted God to do that?

1. Because He is rich in mercy. vs. 4

2. Because of the great love He has for us. vs. 4

CHAPTER 2

3. So that in the ages to come, He might demonstrate to all who might question His justice—the immeasurable riches of His grace and kindness. vs. 7

Making spiritually dead people spiritually alive requires a lot of spiritual power. What **kind** of "power" did God use to accomplish this miraculous transition from spiritual death to spiritual life?

1. The **power** of **grace**. vs. 5
2. The **power** of "**life**" that raised Jesus from the dead. vs. 5—(that "power" is Jesus.) "In Him was **LIFE** and the **LIFE** was the light of men." John 1: 4
3. The **power** of our **faith**—which is His gift. vs. 8

His **purpose** in "making us alive" was to display His workmanship. Another purpose was to bring honor to the Son through the *good works* that spiritually alive people perform because that is what God designed and empowered them to do.

In verses 5 and 8 Paul strongly affirms the salvation by grace principle. "Salvation by grace" means that salvation—*by its nature*—cannot be earned or deserved. If we can do nothing to earn or deserve it, does that mean that salvation—or grace itself—is "unconditional?" Please notice that if salvation by grace is unconditional, it means that **all people** are saved by definition. If salvation by grace is unconditional, it means that preaching, teaching, assembling with the saints, giving of our means, praying, morality, kindness, righteousness, and even believing that Jesus is the Son of God has no bearing on a person's salvation. It also means that every deed done in God's name has no efficacy at all.

Although salvation by grace means that good works have no **saving merit**, it does not mean that they have **no merit at all**. It does not mean that they are unimportant—or even that they have no "influence" on our salvation.

We simply cannot afford to willfully ignore some clear and consistent biblical teachings. In Revelation 20:11-13 the Apostle John says, "Then I saw a great white throne and Him who sat upon it, from whose presence earth and heaven fled away, and no place was found for them. And I saw the dead, the great and the small, standing before the throne, and books were opened; and another book was opened, which is [the book] of life; and the dead were judged from the things which were written in the books, **according to their deeds**. And the sea gave up the dead which were in it, and death and Hades gave up the dead which were in them; and they were judged, every one [of them] **according to their deeds**."

In Matthew 25, when Jesus tells the "Parable of The Virgins," we might ask, "Why were the foolish virgins lost?" The answer is, they were lost because they did not **prepare**. Is "preparation" not a work? Why didn't grace save them?

In the parable of the rich ruler in Mark 10, why was he lost? If we answer that he was lost because he didn't love God enough to **sell** his possessions, **give** them to the poor and **follow** Jesus, do we not have to admit that everything he was asked to **do** constituted "working"? I **do not say** that only "doing" what Jesus told him to do would save him. I **do say** that the foundational reason he was lost was because he didn't love God enough to do them.

In the parable of the talents, recorded in Mathew 25, why was the one talented man condemned? Was it not because he "did" nothing? In that same chapter, we find the vision of judgment. We need to ask on what basis God condemned the "goats." The answer is that He condemned them because they **gave** no water, no food, no clothes, and **made** no visits. Are not all of those things properly classified as "works"? God's grace was not sufficient to save any of those people.

In Revelation 2:23 John records the words of Jesus to the congregation at Thyatira as follows: "I am He who searches the minds and hearts, and I will give to each one of you **according to your deeds**." In Acts 26:20; Paul says; "I preached that they should repent and turn to God and demonstrate their repentance **by their deeds**" (NIV).

Please notice that even this passage from Ephesians 2 concludes with this reminder: "For we are His workmanship, **created** in Christ Jesus **for good works**, which God prepared beforehand so that we would walk in them" (v. 10). My point is that **good works do not create righteousness—righteousness creates good works**. Good works are the natural result of the indwelling divine nature—the Holy Spirit. Good works are **indirectly** essential to salvation because they are the "sign" of what has taken place in our hearts.

In verse 8 Paul says that faith is "the gift of God." Paul means that our ability to believe is a gift from God because He created that ability in us.

Questions Over Ephesians 2:1-10

1. Paul reminds the Christians in Ephesus there was a time when they were "dead." What does he mean by that and what caused that "death?"
2. Does that mean that we were all in that condition at one time? If so, how should that affect our attitude toward those we meet who are in the same condition?
3. What does it mean to "live in sin?"
4. How many of your sins do you think you commit out of ignorance, i.e. you just didn't know better?
5. What is an "object of wrath?" Have you ever thought of yourself as one?
6. What does it mean to be, *"by nature* objects of wrath?"
7. Who or what is the "Spirit" now at work in those who are disobedient?

8. What was God's **purpose** in making the Christians in Ephesus "alive?" Does He have the same purpose when He makes us "alive?"
9. The Christians in Ephesus are no longer spiritually dead, hence no longer objects of wrath. How and when did this change take place?
10. What does "salvation by grace" mean?
11. Does it mean that salvation is "unconditional?"
12. What role—if any—do good works play in salvation?
13. In what way is "faith" a "gift from God?"

---

¹¹"Therefore remember, that formerly you, the Gentiles in the flesh, who are called "Uncircumcision" by the so-called "Circumcision," [which is] performed in the flesh by human hands —¹²[remember] that you were at that time separate from Christ, excluded from the commonwealth of Israel, and strangers to the covenants of promise, having no hope and without God in the world. ¹³But now in Christ Jesus you who formerly were far off have been brought near by the blood of Christ."
(Ephesians 2:11-13)

The congregation in Ephesus was predominantly Gentile. They were unfamiliar with Jewish history, which means that not only were they unfamiliar with the Levitical laws and traditions, they were unfamiliar with the "one God" concept. As pagans they had no idea what it meant to be "under covenant" with God. Their "gods" were feeble by comparison with Jehovah. They were merely glorified, super humans with human desires and human failures. They were not all-knowing, all-loving, all-merciful, all just, all wise, nor all powerful. The God of Abraham, Isaac, and Jacob was a totally new experience for them. He was the God of all creation—close, personal, loving, and could not be contained

CHAPTER 2

or represented in a man-made idol. They had never known a truly holy and divine God who had no human failings nor fleshly desires, a God of compassion and justice, One who was truly interested in them.

In Ephesians 2:11, Paul encourages these Christians to "remember." He wants them to think back and experience again what it was like when they were derisively thought of as, "uncircumcised dogs" by the Jews. He makes a specific reference to their former "un-circumcision" because circumcision was the objective, physical sign that assured the Jews of their covenant relationship with God.

Paul makes a play on words by referring to the Ephesians as—"Gentiles by *birth*." He means that they were Gentiles because they were born to Gentile parents. He draws a parallel between the Gentiles' *physical birth* and the Jews' physical birth. Being "born" a Gentile meant that you **were not** under covenant with God—not one of His "chosen people." Being "born" to Jewish parents meant that you **were** under covenant with God and one of His chosen people. Paul's emphasis is on the implications and ramifications of the "family" into which you were "born."

The conclusion that he draws from this flashback is that, at that time, the time before they accepted Jesus, they were "without Christ," "aliens from the commonwealth of Israel," "strangers to the covenants of promise," "having no hope," and "without God in the world."

I pause for a moment to point out—in deference to those who feel that we have no business "judging" either a person's relationship with God or their eternal destination—that Paul does not hesitate to do so. There is not a single disclaimer, not one hint of a possible exception due to extenuating circumstances in Paul's analysis of the Gentiles' spiritual condition.

Paul's statement that they "have no hope" is uncompromising. Having **no** hope means that *all possibilities* of changing their current spiritual circumstances have been eliminated. Even prayer contains no remedy for the Gentile plight. There is no chance that God will intervene in some "miraculous" way to circumvent their eternal destruction, because they not only have no hope, they are **without God.**

That is the bad news. Paul hastens to remind them of the good news. In verse 13, he says, "but now." It's like waking up from a bad dream to the glorious realization that it was just that—a bad dream—and as **real** as the dream seemed to be, the **greater reality** is that the "Son has risen," and the light of redemptive grace, made possible by His crucifixion and resurrection from the dead, brings renewed hope.

What an inexpressible joy these Gentile Christians must have felt in this poignant reminder of the *despair* of their former state and the *hope* of their present one! There is a *direct and proportional relationship* between the depth of a person's *despair* because of his awareness of his previous condemnation and the height of never-ending *gratitude* and *joy* he experiences in the sublime realization of God's redemption. As the first increases or diminishes, the second increases or diminishes. And so Paul says, "In Christ Jesus, you who once were far off have been brought near **by the blood of Christ**" (Ephesians 2:13, NIV). Remember that the name *Christ* has to do with *the Christ*. In Matthew 16:16, when Jesus asks His disciples who they believe Him to be, Peter, in his historic response answers, "You are **the** Christ, **the** Son of the living God."

There is a direct connection between Paul's emphasis on their being "Gentiles by birth" which meant that they were "far off" (from God)—and his calling their attention to the fact that they have now been "brought near—by the **blood of Jesus.**" The "blood of Jesus" became their right of passage into the family of God when they were **born from above** by the Holy Spirit in the water of baptism. Just as they were without God, strangers

CHAPTER 2

to the covenant and without hope of that ever changing because of their physical birth, their having been spiritually born from above brought them into a spiritual parent-child relationship with God as their Father.

Being "far off" means that they were distanced from God by sin. There is no distance as great as the distance between being lost and being saved, and they had no method of transportation that would shorten that distance. The "vehicle" that God **graciously** provided to bridge the insurmountable distance between their lostness and their salvation by bringing them near was the blood of Jesus.

There can be no reconciliation unless there is first separation. Sin separates us from God. Paul makes this point clearly in Romans 5:10 when he says; "For if while we were enemies, we were reconciled to God through the death of His Son, **much more**, having been reconciled, we shall be saved by His life." And in Colossians 1:22 he says, "...yet He has now reconciled you in His fleshly body through death, in order to present you before Him holy and blameless and beyond reproach." Some translations use the phrase "free from accusation."

They are "free from "accusation" because Satan is the great **accuser.** In Zechariah, 3:1 we read, "Then he showed me Joshua the high priest standing before the angel of the LORD, and Satan standing at his right side to *accuse him.*" In Job 1:9,11, Satan says to God, "Does Job fear God for nothing? Strike everything he has, and he will surely curse you to your face" (NIV). That is Satan's accusation.

Notice especially that reconciliation has taken place *in* Christ's body and *through* his death. These are two deep spiritual concepts tied closely together. First, the concept of the physical death sacrifice of Jesus, the "lamb of God," followed by His glorious triumph over death—resurrection; second, the concept of the "new birth" in which we die spiritually to our old life and are spiritually *resurrected* to a new life. In that new life, we are "born" into the family of God, which is The Church—*Christ's body*. Remember what Paul wrote in Ephesians 1:22-23, "And God placed all things under His feet and appointed Him to be head over everything for *the Church*, which is *His body*, the fullness of Him who fills everything in every way" (NIV). Again in Ephesians 5:23: "For the husband is the head of the wife as Christ is the head of the *Church, His body*, of which He is the Savior" (NIV).

The concept and implications of reconciliation are taken a step further in the following two passages from 2 Corinthians: "All this is from God, who *reconciled us* to Himself *through Christ* and *gave us* the ministry of reconciliation" (5:18, NIV) and "We are therefore Christ's ambassadors, as though *God* were making His appeal *through us*. We implore you on Christ's behalf: Be reconciled to God" (5:20, NIV).

Because God has graciously reconciled us to Himself through Jesus, He has placed on our shoulders the burden of "reconciling" others to God. God makes "His appeal" to the lost through us. That is a sobering thought and places the eternal destiny of others in our hands.

I don't want to leave this thought without pointing out one other passage: "For we do not *preach ourselves*, but Christ Jesus as Lord, and ourselves as your bond-servants for Jesus' sake. For God, who said, 'Light shall shine out of darkness' is the One who has shone in our hearts to give the light of the knowledge of the glory of God in the face of Christ. But we have this treasure in earthen vessels, so that the surpassing greatness of the power will be of God and not from ourselves" (2 Corinthians 4:5-7).

My point in calling this passage to your attention is that though we bear a great responsibility in this business of reconciliation, we need to also be aware of the fact that God, through the Holy Spirit, is equipping us to do the work. Let's look at two more passages that give further impetus to this thought.

In 2 Corinthians 2:16 Paul asks, "Who is sufficient for these

CHAPTER 2

things?" (NKJV) He answers that question in 2 Corinthians 3:4, "Such confidence we have through Christ toward God. Not that we are adequate in ourselves to consider anything as coming from ourselves, but our adequacy is from God, who also made us adequate as servants of a new covenant, not of the letter but of the Spirit; for the letter kills, but the Spirit gives life."

Questions Over Ephesians 2:11-13

1. What were the main differences between the Hebrew God and the "gods" of the pagans?
2. What is the significance of Paul's statement that the Gentiles were "Gentiles by *birth*?"
3. Paul does not hesitate to judge the Gentile's relationship with God or their eternal destination. What can we learn from that?
4. What does "having no hope" mean?
5. After he gives them the "bad news," what "good news" does he give them?
6. For discussion—"There is a *direct and proportional relationship* between the depth of a person's *despair*, because of their awareness of their previous condemnation and the height of the never ending *gratitude* and *joy* they experience in the sublime realization of God's redemption. As the first increases, or diminishes, the second increases, or diminishes."
7. Who is the great accuser? Of what does he accuse us?
8. What does "far off" mean?
9. What "vehicle" does God **graciously** provide to bridge the insurmountable distance between a person's lostness and their salvation.
10. God has given us the "ministry of reconciliation." What does that mean to you?
11. Discuss the idea that there can be no "reconciliation" unless there is first "separation."

12. What is the Holy Spirit's role in reconciliation?
13. Where does reconciliation take place?

¹⁴"For He Himself is our peace, who made both [groups into] one, and broke down the barrier of the dividing wall, ¹⁵by abolishing in His flesh the enmity, [which is] the Law of commandments [contained] in ordinances, so that in Himself He might make the two into one new man, [thus] establishing peace, ¹⁶and might reconcile them both in one body to God through the cross, by it having put to death the enmity. ¹⁷And He came and preached peace to you who were far away and peace to those who were near; ¹⁸for through Him we both have our access in one Spirit to the Father."
(Ephesians 2:14-18)

"He **is** our peace." Jesus did not **bring** peace to us; He **is** peace to us. First, Jesus is peace because He **provided the means** of breaking down the Jew—Gentile "dividing wall" by abolishing the Law of Moses "in His flesh." Not only did He—"in His flesh"—**provide the means** of breaking down the wall between Jew and Gentile, He provided the means of breaking down the wall between "all" humans—whether racial, environmental, educational, social, financial, or gender. Unfortunately, that doesn't mean that all walls have been broken down. It only means that those walls are broken down between those who accept Him as the Lord of their lives and utilize "the power of the cross," as the means of reconciliation.

Even though the Jews had a covenant relationship with God through circumcision and the Law, neither of those things had brought peace or reconciliation with God. In fact, they had actually brought hostility, not because of any flaw in the Law, but because of the sinful nature of the people who lived under

CHAPTER 2

that Law. The Law only *defined sin*, by revealing the nature and personality of God. The flaw was that once sin was defined, the Law had no power to forgive the sins it defined.

Paul comments on this problem in Romans 7:9-12, by saying; "And I was once alive apart from the Law; but when the commandment came, sin became alive, and I died; and this commandment, which was to result in life, proved to result in death for me; for sin, taking opportunity through the commandment, deceived me, and through it killed me. So then, the Law is holy, and the commandment is holy and righteous and good." Paul says that even though the commandment was holy, righteous and good, it had a weakness.

The Hebrew author makes this observation in Hebrews 8:6-10, "But now He (Jesus) has obtained a more excellent ministry, by as much as He is also the mediator of a *better covenant*, which has been enacted on better promises. For if that first [covenant] had been faultless, there would have been no occasion sought for a second. For finding fault with them, He says, 'Behold days are coming, says the Lord, when I will effect a **new covenant** with the house of Israel and with the house of Judah; **Not like** the covenant which I made with their fathers on the day when I took them by the hand to lead them out of the land of Egypt; for they did not continue in My covenant, and I did not care for them, says the Lord. For this is the covenant that I will make with the house of Israel after those days, says the Lord: **I will put my laws into their minds, and I will write them on their hearts.**'"

Notice that God found fault **with the people**, not with the Law. He decided to rectify the situation by making a new law that would make allowances for and provide a remedy to man's sinful nature.

Questions Over Ephesians 2:14-18

1. What is the difference between "bringing peace" and "being peace?"
2. How does Jesus become our peace?
3. Jesus provided the means to peace, but that doesn't mean that there is peace. Why?
4. What was God's purpose for the Law of Moses?
5. What weakness did the Law of Moses have?
6. What did God do to correct that weakness?
7. Where is God's new covenant law written? What is the significance of that?

¹⁹**"So then you are no longer strangers and aliens, but you are fellow citizens with the saints, and are of God's household, ²⁰having been built upon the foundation of the apostles and prophets, Christ Jesus Himself being the corner [stone,] ²¹in whom the whole building, being fitted together is growing into a holy temple in the Lord; ²²in whom you also are being built together into a dwelling of God in the Spirit."**
(Ephesians 2:19-22)

Consequently means "as a result of." In this case, it is as a result of the fact that Jesus abolished in His flesh the law with its commandments and regulations and established a new covenant. This new covenant was a covenant in the mind and on the heart. It is a covenant that incorporates all aspects of man's character and personality and is *built* on the *foundation* of the gospel that the apostles preached: the teachings, death, burial, and resurrection of Jesus. It is also built on Jesus Christ who is the chief cornerstone of that building.

We might ask if God, who is all-knowing, knew that He was going to make a new law, why did He make the old one?

CHAPTER 2

What purpose did the old law serve? The Holy Spirit anticipates our question perfectly and answers it in Galatians 3:19-24 when He says, "**Why the Law then?** It was **added because of transgressions**, having been ordained through angels by the agency of a mediator, **until the seed would come** to whom the promise had been made. Now a mediator is not for one [party only]; whereas God is [only] one. Is the Law then contrary to the promises of God? May it never be! For if a law had been given which was **able to impart life**, then righteousness would indeed have been based on law. But the Scripture has shut up everyone under sin, so that the promise by faith in Jesus Christ might be given to those who believe. But before faith came, we were kept in custody under the law, being shut up to the faith which was later to be revealed. Therefore the Law has become **our tutor** [to **lead us**] **to Christ**, so that we may be justified by faith."

This passage brings us full circle, right back to Ephesians 2:19-21, "**You** (all those who are God's children through faith) are no longer strangers and aliens, but you are fellow citizens with the saints, and are of God's household, having been built upon the foundation of the apostles and prophets, [with] Christ Jesus Himself being the cornerstone." **In Jesus**, the whole **structure** is joined together.

The structure is the kingdom of God—the Church. The Church is made up of an incredible amalgamation of nationalities, personalities, idiosyncrasies, contradictions, colors, histories, environments, traditions, sinfulness, greed, pride, and selfishness. Despite their common problems, all have a common solution—the cross.

"In Jesus" means that we have been justified by the faith that led us to be **baptized into Him**, which is the **only way** we can get "in Jesus." Being "in Jesus" means that we are "Abraham's offspring" and heirs of all of the promises God made to him. **We** are the **fulfillment** of God's promise to Abraham: "In your seed, *all the nations* of the earth shall be blessed" (Genesis 22:18).

Questions Over Ephesians 2:19-22

1. "Consequently" means "as a result of." In this case, as a result of what?
2. If God knew that He was going to make a new covenant, why did He make the old one?
3. What purposes did the old covenant serve? Why was that necessary?
4. Is the Law contrary to the promises of God?
5. What are the predominant differences between the new covenant and the old covenant?
6. If the Law has become **our tutor** to **lead us to Christ**, does that mean that it is critically important that we study and understand the Law?
7. All people have a common problem and a common solution. What are they?
8. Being "in Jesus" means that we are Abraham's offspring. What is the significance of that?
9. How does a person get "in Jesus?"
10. The Church is also the kingdom of God. Does God have more than one kingdom? If we say *no*, why do we talk about there being more than one Church?

(* *Notes on core values*)

It has become evident to me that all human behavior, conduct, moral values, personal identity, and decision-making criteria are based in a person's core values. Those core values begin to be formed early in life. They are influenced by many things, parents, other family members, peers, circumstances, environment, observations, appetites, genetic makeup, social standards, school instructors, and in modern circumstances—disproportionally and negatively by media influences.

If a person's core values are made up of loose, fallible, mixed, or opposing criteria when strong external circumstances coupled

CHAPTER 2

with internal desires that appeal to our senses present themselves, they can be readily violated or even disregarded without feeling guilt, shame, or a need for change or forgiveness.

The most common "natural and material" core value we have is one that, if unrestrained, completely overshadows all others. We inherit it both genetically and environmentally because we witness it in all of the potential influences mentioned above. It is called **self-absorption**. Its foundational motivation leads us to pursue, above all other considerations, what might be described as happiness or more specifically, "our happiness," even more specifically "our happiness right now."

We are all faced with the necessity of making decisions every day about how people and circumstances are going to affect our lives and happiness. Generally speaking, we are naturally predisposed to choosing and making decisions that will satisfy our core value of self-absorption to the exclusion of any other values we might have.

For instance, let's say that a person has a core value of basic honesty and is faced with a situation where being honest will lead to strong negative consequences. However, it would lead to a positive consequence for someone else. The strength of that person's primary self-absorption core value will allow him to violate his secondary "honesty" core value without feeling guilt, because honesty is only a core value *if it serves the self-absorption value*. He doesn't think of himself as acting "selfishly," in a negative sense, because acting in accord with "what is good for me" is a positive quality in a self-absorbed value system.

Since he has no higher and *infallibly right* "standard" by which to judge the "rightness or wrongness" of his criteria for personal happiness, his actions are self justified. Even when his choices hurt others, he justifies it by telling himself that he is simply following the same "natural laws of survival and nature" that everyone else follows and if the situation were reversed, the other person would have made the same decision that he made.

However, if a person's foundational core value comes to be based on unalterable, unchanging, immutable rules of right and wrong that come from an infallible source, that core value will replace the self-absorption core value and will trump all other values connected to it.

For instance, if a person's self-absorption core value comes into direct conflict with its antithesis—"other absorption"—and he chooses the antithesis—the entire foundation of his life is destroyed and every core value he has—no matter what its source, or how deeply ingrained it might be in his conscience is demolished.

Faith in God, as He has revealed Himself, means that He has forever established in the Bible unalterable standards of not just right and wrong *conduct*—but more importantly—right and wrong *thinking*. From the moment a person confesses faith in God, his every thought and every decision must be subjected to the core value "other absorption" test and either be accepted or rejected based on what God has revealed.

External circumstances and deep-seated internal values and desires do not change the "other absorption" core value and even though a person will violate those infallible source core values, he will not seek to find justification or rationale for his actions; instead, he will feel guilt, remorse, shame, and a need for forgiveness. He will also pray fervently for the **power** to overcome any thought process that is in violation of the standards he now accepts as truth.

EPHESIANS
CHAPTER 3

¹"For this reason I, Paul, the prisoner of Christ Jesus for the sake of you Gentiles—²if indeed you have heard of the stewardship of God's grace which was given to me for you; ³that by revelation there was made known to me the mystery, as I wrote before in brief. ⁴By referring to this, when you read you can understand my insight into the mystery of Christ, ⁵which in other generations was not made known to the sons of men, as it has now been revealed to His holy apostles and prophets in the Spirit; ⁶[to be specific,] that the Gentiles are fellow heirs and fellow members of the body, and fellow partakers of the promise in Christ Jesus through the gospel,"
(Ephesians 3:1-6)

Paul didn't believe that he was in prison because of bad actions or bad luck. He was so aware of God's **providential working** in his life that he looked for God in every circumstance. He spoke of his conversion experience—that divine, providential, life-changing intervention on the road to Damascus—as "the administration of God's grace" to him. It was by grace, because Saul had done nothing to deserve it, he was not seeking it. In fact, all of his theological training led him to be opposed to the whole concept of grace.

The nature of what conversion means—the radical alteration of the entire circumference of a person's character, personality, core values, habits, worldview, and purpose in life—requires a providential, mysterious, even "supernatural" intervention.

Paul did not whine or complain about his circumstances. He saw all of his circumstances as *opportunities* to bring glory to God. He was convinced that God had placed him in those circumstances **for that purpose**, because he knew that God would work for good in all circumstances, if he were open to His leading.

God's desire that salvation by grace be proclaimed to the Gentiles had been revealed to Paul. That gave him insight into and understanding of what has been, up to that time, a mystery. The mystery was how God would fulfill His promise to Abraham that in his seed all nations were to be blessed. God chose to use Paul, not only to *reveal* that mystery, but to *administer* it—to put it into actual practice. He saw his imprisonment as God's "providential" wisdom and power at work to implement his ministry to them. (See notes on Ephesians 1:9.)

Paul's assignment was to explain God's mystery, which was that God had fulfilled His promise to Abraham through—of all things—the murder of His Son on a Roman cross. Just as each succeeding generation has tended more and more to minimize and failed to appreciate the import of the War Between the States, modern Christians have tended to minimize the "mystery" that Paul spoke of because they have failed to appreciate the import, the ramifications of this aspect of the gospel. What would have happened if the South had won? Where would we "Gentiles" be if Jesus had not come?

The revelation of the mystery didn't come to Saul on the road to Damascus; that came later. What came **first** to Saul and what has to come first to all who would come to God is the revelation of the Christ Himself. For Saul, that revelation came with a blinding flash of physical light. Sometimes God has to do something really extraordinary to get our attention. That "vision" expanded as he drew closer to God in succeeding years. It is

CHAPTER 3

important to note that Saul's knowledge of the law, his devotion to Moses, and his historical environment all contributed heavily to his enlightenment.

Saul was not a blank piece of paper on the Damascus road. God had been *preparing* this "vessel" for service, long before the vessel became aware of who God was and what His purposes were. The same thing is true of every person whom God calls. Saul had some incredibly important core values when the Damascus road experience took place. Without those values, it could not have taken place in the way it did, because Saul would have had no frame of reference to understand it. His "Who are You, Lord?" (Acts 9:5) question was based on his years of studying how God had revealed Himself to the Jews.

In Ephesians 3:5, Paul reminds his readers that God's plan of redemption was a mystery to all preceding generations and the only reason why he and the other apostles could explain it was because the Holy Spirit had "revealed it" to them. This idea is amplified by what he writes in 1 Corinthians 2:9-10, "Just as it is written, 'Things which eye has not seen and ear not heard, and which have not entered the heart of man, all that God has prepared for those who love Him.' For to us God revealed them through the Spirit; for the Spirit searches all things, even the depths of God."

Peter adds his commentary to this topic in 1 Peter 1:10-12, "As to this salvation, the prophets who prophesied of the grace that [would come] to you made careful search and inquiries, seeking to know what person or time the Spirit of Christ within them was indicating as He predicted the sufferings of Christ and the glories to follow. It was revealed to them that they were not serving themselves, but you, in these things which now have been announced to you through those who preached the gospel to you by the Holy Spirit sent from heaven—things into which angels long to look."

In Ephesians 3:6, Paul stated the mystery clearly, "...the Gentiles are fellow **heirs** and fellow members of the body, and fellow partakers of the promise in Christ Jesus through the gospel." *Heirs* is a critical word because it takes us back to the "descendants of Abraham promise," which had always been understood to refer to his *physical* descendants. God has now revealed that His promise was actually to those who are Abraham's "faith" descendents—not just his physical lineage. This idea springs to life in the conversation between Jesus and Nicodemus in John 3:5, when Jesus announces for the first time the "born again—of water and Spirit" aspect of entering the kingdom of God—rather than the "born-to-Jewish parents circumcision" concept, as the fulfillment of His promise to Abraham.

God promised Abraham that his descendants would be as numerous as the stars. He also promised that through his lineage the "seed" would come. Paul comments on the significance of that "seed" in Galatians 3:16, "Now the **promises** were spoken to Abraham and **to his seed**. He does not say, 'And to **seeds**,' as [referring] to many, but [rather] to **one**, "And to your seed," that is, **Christ**."

The promises God made to Abraham had both physical and spiritual implications. Obviously, the supernatural, physical birth of Isaac and the development of the nation of Israel under God's direct providence fulfilled the physical aspect of the covenant. But it was the spiritual implication of the miraculous birth of the Christ-child and the subsequent proclamation of the gospel that turned out to be the most significant aspect of that covenant.

In Galatians 3:6-9 Paul encourages the Christians in Galatia to consider Abraham: "'[He] believed God, and it was credited to him as righteousness.' Understand, then, **that those who have faith** are **children of Abraham**. Scripture foresaw that God would justify the Gentiles by faith, and announced the gospel in advance to Abraham: '**All nations** will be blessed through you.'

So **those who rely on faith** are blessed along with Abraham, the man of faith" (NIV).

The coming of the Law did not satisfy the "all nations" aspect of the covenant promise. That part was only satisfied in the coming of God's Messiah—the Christ. I seriously doubt that even Abraham himself, much less later generations of Israelites, understood the significance of the "all nations" aspect of the promise. This is evidenced in Galatians 3:13-14 where Paul writes, "Christ redeemed us from the curse of the law by becoming a curse for us, for it is written: 'Cursed is everyone who is hung on a pole.' He redeemed us in order that *the blessing given to Abraham* might come to the Gentiles through Christ Jesus, so that by faith we might receive the promise of the Spirit" (NIV).

Another startling and revolutionary statement that established a new and spiritual definition of what it means to be a Jew and a descendant of Abraham was given by Paul in Romans 2:28-29, "For he is not a Jew who is one outwardly, nor is circumcision that which is outward in the flesh. But he is a Jew who is one inwardly; and circumcision is that which is of the heart, by the Spirit, not by the letter; and his praise is not from men, but from God."

Statements like that allow us to understand why the Jewish leaders hated Paul and wanted him killed. Paul says that Abraham's spiritual descendants are not defined by who their parents are—but by **their faith**. By "faith" they become "children of the **promise**"—not "children of the **flesh**." Their birth is a birth of "water and Spirit" not a birth due to biological principles.

Questions Over Ephesians 3:1-6

1. Why does Paul believe that he is in prison?
2. Paul does not "whine and complain" about his negative circumstances because he believes that all of his circumstances are "providential opportunities" to bring

glory to God. What do you believe about your circumstances positive or negative? Do you use them to glorify God?

3. Name some of Saul's "core values or beliefs" that made the Damascus road experience possible.
4. Do you believe that all "conversions" have a providential, mysterious, life-changing, even supernatural element to them? Can you see those things in your own? Talk about them.
5. What mystery did God make known through the apostles and prophets? How did He do that?
6. God was *preparing* Saul of Tarsus for His service, long before Saul became aware of God's purposes. Do you believe that God has been and is preparing you for His service?
7. The promises to Abraham had both physical and spiritual implications. What were they?
8. What aspect of God's covenant with Abraham was not satisfied by the coming of the Law?
9. What revolutionary way does Paul use to define who a Jew is? Does that make you a Jew?

[7]"…of which I was made a minister, according to the gift of God's grace which was given to me according to the working of His power. [8] To me, the very least of all saints, this grace was given, to preach to the Gentiles the unfathomable riches of Christ, [9] and to bring to light what is the administration of the mystery which for ages has been hidden in God who created all things; [10] so that the manifold wisdom of God might now be made known through the church to the rulers and the authorities in the heavenly [places.] [11] [This was] in accordance with the eternal purpose which He carried out in Christ Jesus our Lord, [12] in whom we have boldness and confident access through faith in Him. [13] Therefore I ask you not to lose heart at my tribulations on your behalf, for they are your glory."
(Ephesians 3:7-13)

CHAPTER 3

In this paragraph, Paul speaks of the eternal purpose that God has carried out in Christ Jesus our Lord. We need to remember that it was always God's plan to redeem mankind—not just the physical descendants of Abraham. Because of the Garden of Eden fall, peace between God and His creation was lost. God determined at that time to restore what was lost there by reconciling mankind to Himself to restore that peace. How He was going to do that was a mystery for centuries—a mystery revealed only in Christ.

God has never revealed the "whys" of His plan and not too many of the "hows." We do know that His plan reached its final stage on the cross and in the resurrection. Paul begins this paragraph with, "Of this **gospel** (the gospel of the cross) I have become a servant, according to the gift of God's grace that was given me by the working of His power."

I am always humbled by the way Paul speaks of himself. He is always so careful to give God the glory and to make sure that his audience is aware that he is nothing in himself. If only to God all of us who have taken up the burden of proclaiming the gospel had his attitude. He refers to himself as a "servant" of the gospel—as the "least of all the saints." He speaks of his commission being "by grace." He constantly elevates and draws attention to the message and demeans himself.

Paul also makes it plain in verse 9 that although his personal mission is directed toward the Gentiles, he has a larger goal: to make *everyone* see what is the plan of the mystery. Paul always seeks to bring his fellow Jews under the covenant of grace. I have often wondered if Paul ever had any premonition of what God was going to do with his letters through the work of Holy Spirit. What an incredible impact they have had on the world—Jew and Gentile—for two thousand years!

Paul's reference to "the church" in verse 10 is worth a comment. Because of the presuppositions we bring to Scripture, when we read that verse, we immediately think of a particular congregation—maybe even a particular religious organization. Paul is not referring to a congregation—or to a group of "congregations"—he is referring to the "body of Christ," which is made up of every "born from above" person on earth. Remember the text from Ephesians 1:22-23: "And He put all things in subjection under His feet, and gave Him as head over all things to **the church**, which is **His body**, the fullness of Him who fills all in all."

Paul says that "the church" is the climax of God's plan to display the "rich variety" of His wisdom. The phrase "rich variety" reminds me of the diverse make up of the first-century church. Think about it for a minute: some fishermen, a seller of purple, a sorcerer, a country doctor, a hired soldier, a castrated black accountant, the warden of a jail, a Jewish theologian, some IRS officials, and a leather dyer. Jesus said that the kingdom of God—the church—was like a net let down into the sea—it brings up all kinds of fish.

The **power** that the Church displays to the world is a strange type of power—a power that the world does not understand. The kingdom of God incorporates none of the normal ingredients of power; it holds no physical property; has no central government and wields no physical authority. It has no formal constitution, no hierarchy, offers no physical or financial inducements, has no way of policing its membership, and is made up exclusively of volunteers. The church defies definition. Membership is extended to anyone on what seems to be an extremely ambiguous and subjective basis.

Paul concludes this paragraph by pleading with his audience not to become discouraged with the fact of his imprisonment. Why would they—or we—become discouraged? Perhaps it is because we continue to misunderstand how God works in our lives and what His purposes are. We continue to believe that God has the same sense of justice and fair play that we do; therefore

CHAPTER 3

He rewards the righteous and curses the wicked. Sounds a lot like Job and his friends, doesn't it? The "negative circumstances"—the inexplicable heartbreak, loneliness, and suffering in all of our lives—lead us to question whether or not God really cares about us and wonder why He doesn't answer our prayers in the way that we desire.

Paul already told them in verse one the reason for his imprisonment. It is for "their sake." Now he goes a step further and tells them that his sufferings are "their glory." How do you suppose they understood those statements? How do we understand them? They seem totally irrational and we are prone to agree with Festus' conclusion that Paul's learning has made him delusional.

Is it possible that Paul was trying to find an explanation for why God didn't get him out of prison so that he could go back to doing the "kingdom work" he was doing before this calamity overtook him? We need to remember that Paul was no "super human Christian." He was as subject to depression, heartbreak, and uncertainty as we are. He had feelings of despair, being abandoned, lonely, defeated, and of being rejected.

Perhaps God was showing Paul that his role in the kingdom of God was changing—perhaps it was only because of his imprisonment that He finally had the time to reflect on all of his experiences. Paul was such an energetic, motivated, and consequently always "on-the-go" kind of person, maybe the Spirit had to slow him down physically to create the setting and the atmosphere for revealing to him the things Paul eventually wrote.

Perhaps it was only in this time of quiet, patient reflection and helplessness that Paul began to appreciate that his role in the kingdom was changing. I would point out that that same thing is true for all of us. We also have preconceived notions of exactly how we are supposed to serve God: the role **we** want to play as well as the role we hope doesn't change. Because of age and circumstances, our roles in the kingdom are forced to change continually.

Perhaps it was there in that prison that Paul learned the "contentment" that he wrote about. God has to get us in the right place before He can teach us what He wants us to teach others and to use us in different ways than ever before. We tend to get stuck in one ministry track and when the circumstances of our lives force us out of that track, we either think we are of no more use, or we try to force our way back into the old track, rather than getting into a new one.

This would explain what he meant in Ephesians 3:13 when he wrote that **they** should not be discouraged by his imprisonment, because **he** is not discouraged. He was teaching them to look for God's "providential working" in their own circumstances. They, too, had to learn that it is Jesus who must be glorified, not themselves. They had to be prepared for the coming of their hour of disappointment, loneliness, persecution, struggle, and doubt. They took heart and used their new circumstances as a means to a new ministry.

Questions Over Ephesians 3:7-13

1. What was God's eternal purpose in redemption?
2. When did God decide on a plan to redeem mankind?
3. When did it reach its final stage?
4. What "mystery" was finally revealed to the apostles?
5. In what ways was Paul careful to give God the glory for his ministry?
6. Discuss the rich diversity among the Christians of the first century and ask yourselves if we have that same type of diversity today. If we don't, why not?
7. How does the church display God's wisdom and power to the world?

CHAPTER 3

8. Paul told them in Ephesians 3:1 that the reason for his imprisonment was for *their sake*. Then he went a step further and told them that his sufferings were "their glory." How do you suppose they understood these statements? How do you understand them?
9. Paul pleaded with his audience not to become discouraged with the fact of his imprisonment. Why would they?
10. Why do we often misunderstand how God works in the circumstances of our lives?
11. What happens when our circumstances force us out of the ministry role that we have always occupied?
12. How do we normally react when that happens? How should we react?
13. Do you ever question God's caring—His answers to your prayers—especially when they are not what you want?

¹⁴**"For this reason, I bow my knees before the Father, ¹⁵from whom every family in heaven and on earth derives its name, ¹⁶that He would grant you, according to the riches of His glory, to be strengthened with power through His Spirit in the inner man; ¹⁷so that Christ may dwell in your hearts through faith; [and] that you, being rooted and grounded in love, ¹⁸may be able to comprehend with all the saints what is the breadth and length and height and depth, ¹⁹and to know the love of Christ which surpasses knowledge, that you may be filled up to all the fullness of God."**
(Ephesians 3:14-19)

This paragraph contains Paul's prayer for the Christians in Ephesus. One of the reasons he told them that he was praying for them was simply to encourage them. If you are like me, you know how reassuring it is know that someone is praying for you, especially someone who you believe to be a spiritually focused person. Paul wanted to remind them that God's eternal purpose—reconciliation with mankind—had been accomplished through Jesus and the church. He also wanted these Ephesian Christians to "have power and spiritual insight"—to have Christ "dwelling in their hearts," and to have the "power to grasp" the love of the Christ.

Paul's prayer posture—"I **kneel** before the Father"—raises some challenging questions for us. Generally speaking, our tendency is to understand them as being "figurative" because we are much more **comfortable** with that interpretation. That is, we don't believe that Paul means that he was literally, physically kneeling; he just meant that he was praying with a "humble attitude."

Potential prayer postures are sitting with heads bowed, standing with heads bowed and or hands raised or not raised, kneeling, bowing at the waist, and prostrating ourselves with our faces to the ground. Do you think that some postures are better than others? Is there a correct prayer posture? Do you think that God is more favorably disposed toward those who show reverence and humility in their physical prayer posture?

If we look closely at examples of the large number of postures mentioned in the Old Testament, these two are fairly typical: "Then the man **bowed low** (bowed at the waist or knelt on his knees) and worshiped the LORD" (Genesis 24:26) and "And when they heard that the LORD was concerned about the sons of Israel and that He had seen their affliction, then they **bowed low** and worshiped" (Exodus 4:31).

Prayer/worship posture isn't mentioned as much in the New Testament. In the story of the ten lepers in Luke 17:15-16, Luke says, "Now one of them, when he saw that he had been healed, turned back, glorifying God with a loud voice, and he **fell on his face** at His feet, giving thanks to Him." The tax collector in Jesus' story of the two men who went up to the temple to pray (Luke

CHAPTER 3

18:10-11) "stood" apparently with bowed head. There's also the account in Matthew 15:25 of the Canaanite woman who comes to Jesus, "began to **bow down** before Him, saying, 'Lord, help me!'" The norm in modern Christian assemblies—and probably in most private prayers—is to either stand or sit with bowed head.

It is interesting to me that I can distinctly remember that it was quite common for the men who led prayer to kneel in the congregations in which I grew up, although I do not recall anyone else doing it. I don't remember exactly when they stopped doing that, but I have an idea why. It was a "generational" posture that displayed what they considered "reverence and humility." Unfortunately, my generation apparently discarded it, perhaps because they considered it "showy." My father and mother's generation had a different attitude toward public worship—and toward life—than the generation that followed.

The transition from an emphasis on "external performance"—under The Law—to "internal transformation"—under grace—would indicate that what I would choose to call a "spiritual or attitudinal posture" is more important to God than the physical. Physical humility unlike attitudinal humility *can be* hypocritical, especially in a public setting, although it need not be.

That does not at all mean that physical posture has no value as an indication of reverence, submission and sincerity—especially when praying privately. Obviously, although kneeling and prostration would be the highest indication of those things, they aren't always possible or practical in our public worship. The way we arrange our seating makes it virtually impossible for most people to assume such a posture.

Paul's initial praise to God in Ephesians 3:14 begins with, "From whom every family in heaven and earth takes its name." It's relatively easy to understand the "family on earth" part, as intended to show the all-inclusiveness of God's reign. The gist is plain; all of mankind has its origin in God, but who in the world are these "families in heaven"? Are they angelic beings? Are they the redeemed dead? Is it simply a literary device to show inclusiveness? It seems dishonest to me to just ignore this phrase. I suppose I could try to bluff my way through something that I don't understand. The truth is, if I **had to** make a decision, I would go with the redeemed dead—since angels don't marry or have children. Since I don't **have to** make a decision, I won't.

Several of Paul's prayers have been recorded. I would call your attention to the completely different nature and wording of Paul's prayers and the ones we pray or hear in our assemblies. Please notice **how seldom** Paul prays for physical health, safety, or any other material concern! Currently, that is about all for which I ever hear anyone pray.

Have you ever heard anyone offer a public prayer that God would "strengthen the congregation with power through his Spirit in their inner being, so that Christ may dwell in their hearts through faith"?

Have you ever heard anyone pray that the congregation would be "rooted and established in love and have the power, together with all the saints, to grasp how wide and long and high and deep is the love of Christ"? **Why don't we pray this way?** Why are our prayers so focused on material things and so lacking in spiritual concerns?

Another important lesson to be learned from Paul's prayer is that it takes the focus off **himself** and places it on **Jesus**. His prayer calls their attention to the scope and power of God's love. He prays that God will strengthen them with **power**. But he goes further. He makes his prayer much more practical by telling them not only **where** he wants that strengthening to take place—in their "inner being"—but **the mechanism** by which he hopes that God will accomplish that strengthening—"through His Spirit." Look carefully at the following passages to see the direct connection between the "strengthening," the "power," the "rooted and grounded in love," the "comprehension," and

CHAPTER 3

the "knowing" and "filling" that takes place in the "inner man" through the indwelling Holy Spirit.

Remember that it is the Holy Spirit who creates spiritual life in us through the new birth, and it is through that spiritual life, that God—whose very nature is "spirit"—is able to communicate His will to us. This idea is born out in the following passages.

- 1 Corinthians 2:12: "Now we have received, not the spirit of the world, but the Spirit who is from God, so that we may know the things freely given to us by God."
- 2 Corinthians 1:21-22: "Now it is God who makes both us and you stand firm in Christ. He **anointed** us, set His **seal of ownership** on us, and put **His Spirit** in our hearts as a deposit, **guaranteeing** what is to come" (NIV).
- 1 John 2:26-27: "I am writing these things to you about those who are trying to lead you astray. As for you, the **anointing** you received from him remains in you, and you do not need anyone to teach you. But as His anointing teaches you about all things and as that *anointing* is real, not counterfeit—just as **it** has taught you, remain in Him" (NIV).
- 1 John 4:13: "We know that we abide in Him and He in us, because He has given us of *His Spirit.*"

Paul's prayer is that first, the Holy Spirit will cause Christ to "dwell in their hearts." What effect does the "dwelling" of Jesus have? In John 17:22-23, Jesus says that one effect of His indwelling is that His followers will be "one"—united. A second effect will be that believers will have the "mind of Christ." Christians will **think** and make decisions in the same way that Jesus did. They will value what He valued and love what He loved by serving others as He served others. I would also point out that a heart that is full of Jesus leaves no room for Satan to get a foothold for the purposes of leading us into materialism or self-centeredness.

EPHESIANS

The second aspect of Paul's prayer is that we will "grasp" (get our arms around/comprehend/understand/know/experience) the love of Christ. Obviously, "knowing" the love of Christ is not easy. If it were, we wouldn't need a special dispensation of power from the Holy Spirit to do it.

I must have had some supernaturally inspired way of using the following verses to make an original and brilliant point about something in the previous section of verses when I first attempted to write this book. Unfortunately, I have no idea what that point was, but each time I edit this chapter, I leave them here in the vain hope—at least so far—that one day as I am working on this, I will have an "A-ha" moment and why they are here will come to me in a flash. I guess that I also leave them here in the vain hope that someone who reads this book will make a connection. If not, at least I hope they will make you shake your head and laugh.

The first is from the prologue to Geoffrey Chaucer's *Canterbury Tales*. It has been a number of years since I actually saw it in its original form, so if there happens to be a Chaucer scholar out there, please forgive any misspellings.

> Whan that Aprille with its shoures soote, the droghte of Marche hath perced to the roote and bathed every veyne in swich liquor, of which virtu engendred is the flour; whan Zephirus eek, with his swete breeth, inspired hath in every holt and heeth, the tender croppes, and the yonge son hath in the Ram his halfe cours y-ronne, and smale fowles maken melode, that slepen al the night with open ye, (So pricketh hem nature in hir corages: than longen folk to goon pilgrimages.

The second is from Lewis Carroll's "Jabberwocky."

> Twas brillig, and the slithy toves did gyre and gimble in the wabe. All mimsy were the borogoves, and the mome raths outgrabe.

CHAPTER 3

Questions Over Ephesians 3:14-19

1. What are some of the reasons why Paul not only tells the congregation that he is praying for them, but also for what he is praying?
2. Spend time discussing "prayer posture." Use the following questions as discussion points. Where do you do most of your private praying? Is it a place where you can use different postures, if you feel the need? Do you have a favorite posture in private prayer? Do you think one prayer posture is more correct or indicates more sincerity than another? Do you think that the posture we use in prayer is important to God, especially in private prayer? Do you think that God is more favorably disposed toward those who show reverence and humility in their physical prayer posture?
3. "From whom every family *in heaven* and earth takes its name." Who are these "families in heaven?" If someone really *knows*, please send me an email. (On second thought, don't send me an email.)
4. By what "method or agency" does Paul expect his prayer for them to be answered?
5. Why do you think our prayers so focused on material things (more than 95 percent of all public requests for prayer are for health and safety concerns.) Recently, I was visiting a large urban congregation and read in their bulletin a fervent prayer request for safe travel for a group of missionaries—rather than for the success of the mission! Why are there so few requests for spiritual concerns?
6. Name and discuss some of the things that the indwelling Holy Spirit does in us. How does He do that?
7. What effect does the "dwelling" of Jesus have in our hearts have?

**[20]"Now to Him who is able to do far more abundantly beyond all that we ask or think, according to the power that works within us, [21]to Him [be] the glory in the church and in Christ Jesus to all generations forever and ever. Amen."
(Ephesians 3:20-21)**

The last paragraph of this chapter is Paul's prayer of praise, acknowledgement, faith, and trust. The "power at work" within us can be nothing but the Holy Spirit. His work is guiding us, filling our hearts with the "fruits of the Spirit": joy, hope, peace patience, kindness, and the love of God. He also admonishes, reminds, motivates, convicts, assures, and helps us with our prayers. "To Him"—to the glorious God of our salvation—"be glory in the church"—may all that the body of Jesus our Lord accomplishes bring glory to God—"and in Christ Jesus"—God's glory is manifested in the lifting up of His only begotten Son—"to all generations forever and ever. Amen."

God's *ability* to answer our prayers—"all that we ask or think"—is accomplished through the agency of the *indwelling Spirit*—"the power that works within us." We need to remember that the work of the Holy Spirit is to glorify Jesus, not Himself or us. He glorifies Jesus best, not by empowering people to speak in tongues, perform healing, or produce miraculous signs, but by empowering them to produce the spiritual fruits that result from His indwelling.

The apostle John quotes Jesus in 16:12-15 as saying, "I have many more things to say to you, but you cannot bear them now. But when He, the Spirit of truth, comes, **He** will *guide you* into all truth; for **He** will not speak on his own initiative; but whatever **He** hears, **He** will speak; and He will disclose to you what is to come. **He will glorify Me, for He will take of** mine and will disclose it to you. All things that the Father has are mine; therefore I said **that He** takes of Mine and will disclose it to you."

CHAPTER 3

Questions Over Ephesians 3:20-21

1. One purpose of prayer is seen in Paul's closing words as he praises, glorifies, honors, and pours out thanksgiving to God.
2. How can God accomplish far more than we can imagine?
3. Does that mean that we need to imagine more and ask for more?
4. What is the Spirit's work in us?

EPHESIANS
CHAPTER 4

¹**Therefore, I, the prisoner of the Lord, implore you to walk in a manner worthy of the calling with which you have been called,** ²**with all humility and gentleness, with patience, showing tolerance for one another in love,** ³**being diligent to preserve the unity of the Spirit in the bond of peace.** ⁴**[There is] one body and one Spirit, just as also you were called in one hope of your calling;** ⁵**one Lord, one faith, one baptism,** ⁶**one God and Father of all who is over all and through all and in all.**
(Ephesians 4:1-6)

Paul begins this section of the book by reminding the congregation in Ephesus that he is writing to them from a Roman prison cell. That reminder is directly related to his pleading with them to lead a life that is worthy of their calling. That is exactly how he is trying to conduct himself under trying circumstances. His admonition seems to be, "If I can bear with the injustice of being imprisoned for no reason at all; if I can continue to act as Jesus would have me act; if I can see the providential working of God in these circumstances; you can, too."

Paul's physical perspective gives him spiritual insight into his relationship with Jesus. Just as he is a physical prisoner, held involuntarily by the Romans, he is a spiritual prisoner held in *voluntary* bondage to Jesus. The irony of this is that it was Jesus who freed him from his slavery to sin and self-interest. What is so

75

difficult for us to realize— especially as Americans who think of ourselves as being free—is that we are all prisoners because we are all in bondage to something or someone else. The most common, the most demanding and the most insidious type of bondage is self-interest. There is no tyranny that compares with it on this earth. Satan knows that if we succumb to the seductive power of self-interest, his goal of separating us from God is complete.

In Romans 6:16 Paul writes, "Do you not know that when you present yourselves to someone [as] slaves for obedience, you are slaves of the one whom you obey, either of sin resulting in death, or of obedience resulting in righteousness?" Of course, we do not think of that type of bondage as being quite as serious as physical bondage. It fact, it is much worse because we like it.

"Leading a life that is worthy of our calling" means that our actions, core values, morals, speech, decision-making, and thoughts must be on a level that corresponds to the faith that we profess. It also calls for complete dedication to seeking God's purposes for our life. To be "worthy" implies that there is a direct correlation between the holiness to which God has called us and the practical aspect of our response to that call.

Paul writes to the congregation in Thessalonica in 2 Thessalonians 1:5, "[This is] a plain indication of God's righteous judgment so that you will be **considered worthy** of the kingdom of God, for which indeed you are suffering."

Paul says that worthiness is the result of perseverance and faith in the face of persecutions and trials. In 2 Thessalonians 1:11 he writes, "With this in mind, we constantly pray for you, that our God may count you **worthy** of his calling, and that by **his power** he may bring to fruition your every desire for goodness and your every deed prompted by faith." Note that the "power" by which we become "worthy" comes from God.

Paul defines what he means by being worthy of God's calling by saying that we must have an attitude of "humility;" treat others with "gentleness;" be "patient" with the weak; and "bear

CHAPTER 4

with one another in love;" which allows us to "maintain the unity of the Spirit." Few things either attract or repel outsiders more than the way Christians talk about and treat one another.

I would call your attention to the fact that in no area of our personal lives are we more open to the scrutiny of non-Christians than in our congregational relationships. Talking negatively and in a demeaning way about congregational issues to non-members is fairly common, especially when those to whom we are talking are doing the same thing about their fellowship. Doing that is contrary to the spirit of Christ and leaves a bad impression.

Jesus' teachings in Matthew 5 about the value of being "poor in spirit;" being one of "those who mourn;" being "meek;" being "pure in heart;" and being "peacemakers;" when placed together paint a picture of the model that Christ displayed in His own life. All of those personality traits have in common the idea of one of Jesus' outstanding qualities: gentleness. Please look carefully at the following Scripture references:

- In Matthew 11:28-29, Jesus describes Himself in this way: "Come to me, all you who are weary and burdened, and I will give you rest. Take my yoke upon you and learn from me, for I am **gentle and humble** in heart, and you will find rest for your souls" (NIV).
- Proverbs 15:1: "A **gentle answer** turns away wrath, but a harsh word stirs up anger."
- Proverbs 25:15: "By forebearance a ruler may be persuaded, and a soft [**gentle**] tongue breaks the bone."
- Matthew 21:5: "Say to the Daughter of Zion, 'Behold, your king is coming to you, **gentle** and mounted on a donkey."
- 1 Thessalonians 2:6-7: "Even though as apostles of Christ we might have asserted our authority. But we proved to be **gentle** among you, as a nursing mother tenderly cares for her own childen."

- Gentleness is one of the qualities necessary to be an elder: "The overseer is to be...not violent but **gentle**" (1 Timothy 3:3).

- Although 1 Peter 3:3-4 is directed specifically to wives, the principles found in this passage are descriptive of every person who claims to follow the Christ: "Your beauty should not come from outward adornment, such as elaborate hairstyles and the wearing of gold jewelry or fine clothes. Rather, it should be that of your **inner self**, the unfading beauty of a **gentle and quiet spirit**, which is of great worth in God's sight" (NIV).

Gentleness is the antithesis of pride and arrogance. The quality most essential to acquiring gentleness is genuine humility. Living a life that is "worthy of the calling we have received" is completely dependent on the extent to which we have been molded into the image of the Christ. We cannot say that we have been molded into that image unless we have incorporated the quality of gentleness. We need to ask ourselves if *gentleness* is the word our friends, families, neighbors, and those with whom we work would use to describe us.

The "worthiness" that Paul speaks of is the result of the calling Christians have received. We must ask ourselves to what were we **called**; who did the calling; how did He do it; and what was His purpose?

One of the things we learn from Isaiah 6 is that the first **call** of God is not to "do" but to "know." **Knowing** God is a prerequisite to being able to hear His call. Isaiah could only answer the call of God to serve because he knew the One who was calling him. God is spirit and the process of coming to know God means that there has to be a spiritual awakening—a spiritual birth. That is what Jesus tries to tell Nicodemus in John 3.

The Jews of Jesus' day missed the call of God through His Messiah because they did not know Him: "Then Jesus cried out in

CHAPTER 4

the temple, teaching and saying, 'You both know Me and know where I am from; and I have not come of Myself, but He who sent Me is true, whom you do not know. I know Him, because I am from Him, and He sent me'" (John 7:28-29). Also read John 8:19: "So they were saying to Him, 'Where is Your Father?' Jesus answered, '**You know neither Me nor my Father**; if you knew Me, you would know My Father also."

Paul writes in 2 Thessalonians 2:13-14, "But we should always give thanks to God for you, brethren beloved by the Lord, because God has chosen you from the beginning for salvation through sanctification by the Spirit and faith in the truth. It was for this He **called you** through our **gospel**, that you may gain in the glory of our Lord Jesus Christ." Here we learn that God's "call" comes through the gospel.

Peter writes in 2 Peter 1:3, "His divine power has granted to us everything pertaining to life and godliness, through the true knowledge of Him who **called us** by His own **glory and excellence**." In addition to the gospel, we are called by God's glory and excellence.

Paul, in Romans 8:28 ads this thought, "And we know that God causes all things to work together for good to those who love God, to those who are **called** according to **His purpose**." These verses establish that it is God who calls us and that He calls us in five distinct ways:

1. Through the sanctifying work of the Spirit.
2. Through belief in the truth.
3. Through the gospel.
4. By His own glory and wisdom.
5. According to His purpose.

Consider this from Hebrews 3:1: "Therefore, holy brethren, partakers of a *heavenly calling*, consider Jesus, the Apostle and High Priest of our confession."

Also read this verse from 1 Corinthians "God is faithful, through whom you were *called into fellowship* with His Son, Jesus Christ our Lord" (1:9).

From these passages we learn that our calling is a "heavenly one." We also learn that we are called to be in **fellowship** with Jesus. Being in fellowship with Jesus sounds like a pleasant and reassuring thing, but it is easily overlooked that being in "fellowship with Jesus" means that we must be willing to **suffer** with Him.

Paul writes an intriguing passage on this idea in Colossians 1:24: "Now I rejoice in my sufferings for your sake, and in my flesh I do my share on behalf of His body (which is the church) in filling up that which is **lacking in Christ's afflictions**." The only thing that could possibly "be lacking" in the afflictions of Christ is **our own suffering**. We learn in Hebrews 5:8 that Jesus "learned obedience" through the things that He suffered, but *His* suffering does not teach *us* obedience; we must learn obedience through our own suffering.

Peter writes in 1 Peter 4:12-13, "Beloved, do not be surprised at the fiery ordeal among you, which comes upon you for your testing, as though some strange thing were happening to you; but to the degree that you **share** in the **sufferings of Christ**, keep on rejoicing, so that also at the revelation of His glory you may rejoice with exultation." Being called into fellowship with Jesus means that when we are "in fellowship with Jesus," *we are also in fellowship with every other person who has been called into that fellowship.* That idea has important implications for the criteria we use to define the "boundaries" of kingdom of God.

Now we need to ask, What *did God call us to be or to do*? In Romans 1:1 Paul says that God called him **to be** an apostle. The following passages will tell us much more about this topic that is applicable to everyone.

- 1 Corinthians 1:2: "To the church of God which is at

CHAPTER 4

Corinth, to those who have been sanctified in Christ Jesus, **saints by calling**, with all who in every place call on the name of our Lord Jesus Christ, their [Lord] and ours..." We are **all** called to be saints.

- Galatians 5:13: "For you were **called to freedom**, brethren; only [do] not [turn] your freedom into an opportunity for the flesh, but through love serve one another." We are **all** called to be free from law, free from sin, free from condemnation, and free to love and serve one another.

- 2 Thessalonians. 2:14-15: "It was for this He called you through our gospel, that you may gain the glory of our Lord Jesus Christ. So then, brethren, stand firm and hold to the traditions which you were taught, whether by word [of mouth] or by letter from us." We are **all** called through the gospel. We are **all** called to share in the glory of Jesus. We are **all** called to stand firm and hold to the teachings of the apostles.

- 1 Peter 2:9: "But you are a chosen race, a royal priesthood, a holy nation, a people for God's own possession, so that you may proclaim the excellencies of Him who has **called you** out of darkness into His marvelous light." **All** Christians are called out of darkness into God's light for the purpose of declaring the praises of the One who called us.

- 1 Peter 2:20-21: "For what credit is there if, when you sin and are harshly treated, you endure it with patience? But if when you do what is right and suffer [for it] you patiently endure it, this [finds] favor with God. For you have been **called for this purpose**, since Christ also suffered for you, leaving you an example for you to follow in His steps." We have all been called to bear suffering and injustice bravely, and we have all been called to follow in Jesus' footsteps.

- 1 Peter 3:8-9: "To sum up, let all be harmonious,

sympathetic, brotherly, kindhearted, and humble in spirit; not returning evil for evil, or insult for insult, but giving a blessing instead; for **you were called for the very purpose** that you might inherit a blessing." We are **all** called to live harmonious, sympathetic, brotherly, kindhearted lives and to be humble in spirit, blessing others so that we might in turn be blessed.

- 1 Peter 5:10: "And the God of all grace, who **called you** to his **eternal glory** in Christ, after you have suffered a little while, will himself restore you and make you strong, firm and steadfast" (NIV). We are **all** called to share in Jesus' eternal glory.

Why does Paul admonish the Ephesians to "bear with one another?" The reality of life and relationships is that in spite of our best efforts to make ourselves more "lovable," there is much about even the best of us that simply has to be "put up with." The thing most needed in "bearing with one another" is **humility**—the realization that there is much about us that is less than desirable.

"Unity of the Spirit"

What is the "unity of the Spirit"? Let me call your attention to a passage that we all know well, although we have seldom appreciated the depth of it. In John 3:5-8 Jesus, speaking to Nicodemus says, "Truly, truly, I say to you, unless one is born of water and the Spirit he cannot enter into the kingdom of God. That which is born of the flesh is flesh, and that which is born of the Spirit is spirit. Do not be amazed that I said to you, 'You must be born again.' The wind blows where it wishes and you hear the sound of it, but do not know where it comes from and where it is going; so is everyone who is born of the Spirit."

The "unity of the Spirit" is the oneness every child of God experiences through their "genetic similarities" with every other

CHAPTER 4

person who has been "born of the Spirit." When we were born from above by faith, obedience, and baptism, it was the Holy Spirit who created spiritual life in us—"the Spirit gives birth to spirit." In the new birth we literally become the spiritual children of God. (Since God **is** Spirit, His children must therefore also be spirit.) Because we have a common parent, we have common genetic traits. Second Peter 2:4 tells us that in the new birth we literally take on the "divine nature."

Romans 8:5-6 says, "Those who live according to the flesh have their minds set on what the flesh desires; but those who live in accordance with the Spirit have their minds set on what the Spirit desires. The mind governed by the flesh is death, but the mind **governed by the Spirit** is life and peace." Verses 14-16 explain even further, "because for all who are being led by the Spirit of God these are **sons of God**. For you have not received a spirit of slavery leading to fear again, but you have received a spirit of adoption as sons by which we cry out, 'Abba! Father!' The Spirit Himself testifies with our spirit that we are **children of God**." Here is a short list of the conclusions we can draw from these passages.

1. What the Spirit "desires" is the same for *all of us*, and that leads to unity.
2. Minds *controlled by the same Spirit* are minds united in purpose.
3. Everyone who is "led by the Spirit" is "led" in the same basic direction.

Even beyond these passages, Jude writes in verse 19, that it is people who are "devoid of the Spirit" who cause divisions among God's people.

Unity requires every person involved to "make every effort." Unity does not come naturally to us. What do come naturally are pride, conceit, and selfish ambition—all of which lead to discord. Paul writes to the Roman Christians in 12:16-18, "Be of the same mind toward one another; do not be haughty in mind, but associate with the lowly. Do not be wise in your own estimation. Never pay back evil for evil to anyone. Respect what is right in the sight of all men. If possible, so far as it depends on you, be at peace with all men."

Paul says that being of the same mind—unity—demands that we exercise humility (associating with the lowly and not thinking of ourselves as being smarter than everyone else.) He also says that peace and unity are "everybody's responsibility." We cannot be at peace with those who refuse to do what it takes to have it, unless it is on their terms.

An important part of "making every effort" to have unity among ourselves is that we must discipline ourselves to place the **best possible interpretation** on the words and actions of others. It's interesting that we find that so easy to do with people we like, but when we don't like someone, we tend to place the worst possible interpretation on what they say and do.

I was preaching for a congregation once where there were no elders; hence we had periodic "men's business meetings." (I don't know which is worse.) In one meeting a brother took me to task severely over something I had said in the previous Sunday's sermon. When he got through berating me, another brother spoke up and said that he had heard the same sermon and although he didn't always agree with what I said, he wasn't offended at all. He then added this comment, "The difference between what you heard and what I heard has nothing to do with what John said; it has to do with the fact that I like John, and you don't."

In Ephesians 4:4-6, Paul gives further clarification to how we can have "unity of the Spirit." The "seven ones" are the bedrock of our faith and the foundation upon which the whole Christian system rests. When any of the various doctrines and traditions that make up the superstructure of what we may believe is successfully challenged, we begin to rebuild. So often, I have heard

CHAPTER 4

people say that their faith had been weakened because some treasured doctrine was challenged. We must be careful about the things in which we place our faith.

There are many beliefs that I hold personally dear that are not necessarily the things that my faith *rests upon*. For instance, from the time I was a child, I was taught and firmly believed that all biblical teachings were of equal importance. It was many years later that I had to come to terms with the fact that they are not. I will give you two biblical examples of why they are not.

In 1 Corinthians 15:3-5 Paul writes, "For what I delivered to you as of **first importance** what I also received: that Christ died for our sins according to the Scriptures, and that He was buried, and that He was raised on the third day according to the Scriptures, and that He appeared to Cephas, then to the twelve." If Jesus' death, burial, and resurrection are of "first importance," then there must be other things that are at least second in importance.

A second illustration is found in Matthew 22:36-40 where Matthew records that a man came to Jesus with this question: "Teacher, which is the **great commandment** in the Law?" Matthew says that Jesus replied, "'Love the Lord your God with all your heart, and with all your soul, and with all your mind.' This is the **great** and **foremost** commandment. The second is like it, 'You shall love your neighbor as yourself.' On these two commandments depend the whole Law and the Prophets."

Notice that Jesus does not say, "There is no **greatest** commandment; they are all equal." He says that the first commandment is the greatest—the most important, which means that the others must be less important. Please note that **He does not say** that they are unimportant—only less important—and there is a great deal of difference.

In Matthew 23:23, Jesus states the case perfectly, "Woe to you, scribes and Pharisees, hypocrites! For you tithe mint and dill and cumin, and have neglected the **weightier provisions** of the law: justice and mercy and faithfulness; but these are the things you **should have done, without** neglecting the others."

That means that practicing justice, showing mercy, and maintaining faithfulness are more important than giving a tenth of your spices, but giving a tenth of your spices is still important.

The one body, one Spirit, one hope, one Lord, one faith, one baptism, and one God, are co-dependent truths; each draws its truth from the other and if one should fall, they all fall. Paul's statement that there is one body is true in two senses.

1. First, it is true because the oneness of the body is a necessary consequence of the other "ones."
2. Second, it is true because the physical body of Jesus was by definition a single entity. His body, which is also The Church, is by definition a single entity and cannot be otherwise. Paul asks in 1 Corinthians 1:13, "Is Christ divided?" The question is rhetorical, because it suggests an oxymoron (a contradiction in terms).

I would offer the following comments on each of the "ones."

"One Lord"

The "one Lord" needs little further explication to those of us who have grown up with it. Attempting to discuss how we can believe in the Trinity and believe in the one God concept is beyond the scope of this work. However, I do want to point out that Paul was writing to a congregation where there were many first-generation Christians, many of them Gentiles, who had grown up in a pagan culture where they worshiped a multitude of gods. I'm confident they struggled with the "one God" concept, and Paul found it necessary to reaffirm it.

"One Faith"

Understanding Paul's statement that there is only "one faith"

CHAPTER 4

necessitates our differentiating between *the* faith and personal faith. Please note the following passages that specifically discuss "the faith."

- Acts 6:7: "So the word of God spread. The number of disciples in Jerusalem increased rapidly, and a large number of priests became obedient to **the faith**" (NIV).
- Acts 13:8: "But Elymas the sorcerer (for that is what his name means) opposed them and tried to turn the proconsul from **the faith**" (NIV).
- Acts 14:21-22: "After they had preached the gospel to that city and had made many disciples, they returned to Lystra and to Iconium and to Antioch, strengthening the souls of the disciples, encouraging them to continue in **the faith**."
- 1 Corinthians 16:13: "Be on the alert; stand firm in **the faith**, act like men, be strong."
- 2 Corinthians 13:5: "Test yourselves to see if you are in **the faith**."
- Galatians 1:23: "They kept hearing, He who once persecuted us is now preaching **the faith** which he once tried to destroy."
- 1 Timothy 5:8: "But if anyone does not provide for his own, and especially for those of his immediate household, he has denied **the faith** and is worse than an unbeliever."
- Philippians 1:25–27: "Convinced of this, I know that I will remain, and I will continue with all of you for your progress and joy in **the faith**, so that through my being with you again your boasting in Christ Jesus will abound on account of me. Whatever happens, conduct yourselves in a manner worthy of the gospel of Christ. Then, whether I come and see you or only hear about you in my absence, I will know that you stand firm in one Spirit, striving together as one for **the faith** of the gospel" (NIV).

- 1 Timothy 3:9: "They must keep hold of the deep truths of **the faith** with a clear conscience."
- 1 Timothy 4:1,6: "But the Spirit explicitly says that in later times some will fall away from **the faith**, paying attention to deceitful spirits and doctrines of demons. In pointing out these things to the brethren, you will be a good servant of Christ Jesus, constantly nourished on the words of **the faith** and of the sound doctrine which you have been following."
- Titus 1:12-13: "'Cretans are always liars, evil beasts, lazy gluttons.' This testimony is true. For this reason reprove them severely, so that they may be sound in **the faith**."

From these passages we learn that the "one faith" that Paul talks about is something that can be "obeyed," "turned from," be "true to," "stood firm in," "examined," "preached," "denied," a person can "progress and find joy in," "contend for," contains "deep truths," can be "abandoned," and a person can be "sound" in it.

These passages lead us to the inevitable conclusion that the "one faith" that Paul refers to is the same as "*the* faith" that is mentioned in these passages. We can also conclude that both of these terms refer to an objective and historically verifiable body of teachings, knowledge, and beliefs.

The following passages are just a sample of biblical references to personal faith:

- Romans 1:8,11-12: "First, I thank my God through Jesus Christ for all of you, because **your faith** is being proclaimed throughout the whole world. I long to see you so that I may impart to you some spiritual gift to you, that you may be established; encouraged together by **the other's faith**."
- Romans 14:1-2: "Accept the one **who is weak in faith** but not for the purpose of passing judgment on his opinions.

CHAPTER 4

One person has faith that he may eat all things, but he who is weak eats vegetables only."

- 1 Corinthians 2:4: "My message and my preaching were not in persuasive words of wisdom, but in demonstration of the Spirit and of power, so that **your faith** would not rest on the wisdom of men, but on the power of God."
- 2 Corinthians 10:15: "Our hope is that, as **your faith** continues to grow, our sphere of activity among you will greatly expand" (NIV).

"One Baptism"

How can we harmonize Paul's reference to there being "one baptism" in the light of biblical references to baptism in the Holy Spirit and John's baptism? Dealing with John's baptism is relatively easy since it began and ended under the Law of Moses while Paul refers to an act that is specifically integral to Christianity.

The disagreements that are generated by the baptism—with, in, by, or of the Holy Spirit and the "miraculous" gifts received through the laying on of the apostle's hands center in and around a single issue—are the ability to perform miracles, specifically to speak in tongues (languages unknown to the speaker) and to heal in the way that Jesus and the apostles healed in the first century.

This discussion rests in the highly subjective area of personal interpretation and the appeal it has to human pride, sensationalism, and personal aggrandizement. It also gives credence to the idea that there is a proportional relationship between having miraculous spiritual gifts and being spiritually mature—**there is no such relationship**! The congregation in Corinth where these gifts were most evident—in fact, the only congregation that we know of where they existed—was the most materialistic, divided, and unspiritual congregation that Paul addressed.

The importance and purpose of miraculous gifts and the role they played in the successful proclamation of the gospel in the first century is greatly misunderstood. As they are employed today, they place an inordinate amount of importance on physical health, materialistic (especially, financial) blessings, and the duration of this life, while de-emphasizing the "fruits of the Spirit."

Every person whom Jesus healed—even those whom He raised from the dead—later got sick and died. If the **main purpose** of the miracles of Jesus was to heal and to preserve life, He failed miserably. Neither Jesus, nor His apostles healed every sick person with whom they came in contact. The cripple at the pool in Jerusalem was one of hundreds and as far as the text is concerned, He only healed this one. The significance of Jesus' statement that His kingdom was not of this world has to play a role in our understanding of the role and purpose of miracles.

By the same power that He used to cure sickness, God could have prevented sickness. If the purpose of miracles of healing was to make this earth a place of perfect health and eternal reward, the miracles of Jesus and the apostles again failed miserably.

There can be no doubt that the occurrence of miraculous events in the New Testament declined as The Church became more mature. There can be no doubt that the tone of Paul's comments in 1 Corinthians 12-14 is decidedly negative about the intrinsic and extrinsic value of miraculous spiritual gifts. Evidences of possible modern-day miracles, especially speaking in tongues and healing, are universally suspect and are never either as consistent or conclusive as they were in the New Testament. There seems to be a different understanding of the nature of tongue speaking as it was evidenced in New Testament times and as it is commonly evidenced today.

My conclusions are as follows:

1. Baptism in, by, of, or through the Holy Spirit is a different ministration of the Spirit, not connected to the baptism in water that is an integral part of the New Birth.

CHAPTER 4

2. Baptism in the Holy Spirit is **similar** in how it was imparted and in its effect, to the "filled with the Holy Spirit" of the Old Testament and the New Testament. It is therefore an action taken by God **solely at His discretion**, which He may choose to impart again whenever His purposes would be served. If the question is, "Does God still have the power to give people the ability to speak in foreign languages and can He still heal people miraculously through the hands of people He chooses?"; I hope I don't need to answer that question. **Of course He can.** The question that remains is, "Does He?"

3. Since we can do absolutely nothing to receive this baptism and these "gifts," it is foolish, counterproductive, and immature for us to dispute this topic.

4. Every promise that relates to the work of the Holy Spirit within the Christian is unquestionably at our disposal with the notable exception of being the "agent" through whom miracles are performed.

5. This does not mean that the performance or occurrence of miracles in modern times is in doubt. There can simply be no question about the willingness of God to intervene supernaturally in the lives of His saints. He also intervenes supernaturally in every day events to bring His purposes to pass. It does mean that the working of those miracles through the specific action of human agents is in serious doubt.

6. This **in no way** limits the power of prayer or the ability of human beings to influence supernatural intervention through their petitions. It only means that God's responses are not identified with a human agency.

(* *For a more detailed discussion of this topic, please see the notes on page 119.*)

Questions Over Ephesians 4:1-6

1. What does it mean for those of us who are living in this culture to "live a life that is worthy of the calling we have received?"
2. What is the calling we have received?
3. Who has called us?
4. How were we called?
5. What was His purpose in calling us?
6. Are all commandments of equal importance?
7. What does it mean to "bear with one another?"
8. What *quality* is most needed to be able to "bear with one another?"
9. What is "unity of the Spirit" and how do we achieve it?
10. What is the difference between *the faith* and personal faith?
11. How can we harmonize Paul's reference to there being "one baptism" in the light of biblical references to baptism in the Holy Spirit and John's baptism?

⁷"But to each one of us grace was given according to the measure of Christ's gift. ⁸Therefore it says, 'When He ascended on high, He led captive a host of captives, and He gave gifts to men.' ⁹(Now this [expression,] 'He ascended,' what does it mean except that He also had descended into the lower parts of the earth? ¹⁰He who descended is Himself also He who ascended far above all the heavens, that He might fill all things.)"
(Ephesians 4:7-10)

In verses 1-6 Paul establishes the foundation for unity by focusing the reader's attention on the "ones." In this section, he turns his attention to the foundation of every human being's relationship

CHAPTER 4

with God—grace. Paul says that mankind receives grace, "according to the measure of Christ's gift."

Christ's "gift" reached its culmination on the cross, but it didn't *originate* there. It didn't even originate with His birth in Bethlehem of Judea. It originated in heaven, when He volunteered to surrender His divinity—His unlimited and purely "Son of God" status—and take on the *additional* limited and finite qualities of Son of Man status by being born in Bethlehem of Judea. Jesus didn't just surrender His Son of Man life for our sakes—hundreds of thousands of people have died for other people—Jesus surrendered His Son of God and Son of Man life—something no one has ever done or ever will do.

That means that the depth of His sacrifice cannot be measured by any human scale. The reason behind the unique nature of His infinite sacrifice was that mankind's debt of sin against God was infinite, and they had nothing to offer as payment, so the only way the infinite debt could be paid was by an infinite amount of grace. The grace that paid that debt was measured out according to the infinite dimensions of the cross.

There is a rich variety in God's application of grace. Some aspects of it are "universal and continuous," that is, they have no inherent relationship to a person's lifestyle, faith, morality, or even to their salvation. For instance, physical life itself is a gift of grace that is "measured out" to every human being regardless of where or how they live. Every aspect of what we call "nature"—from sunshine, rainfall, seasons, rivers, deserts, and trees to mountains and oceans—all are gifts of grace from a loving Father. Even the air we breathe is a gift of grace, and all receive it equally—although all are not equally grateful.

The grace involved in God's providential intervention in the lives of people and His response to their prayers is *not* "measured out" equally, but is distributed to individuals solely on the basis of His "divine discretion."

The grace involved in Jesus' "leading a host of captives captive" when He ascended into heaven is God's "saving grace," which is not "measured out" equally to all, but only to those "sin-laden captives" who have confessed their faith in the risen Christ as the Son of God and have been born from above in baptism as a response to the gospel of grace. But there is yet another kind of grace.

Beginning in Ephesians 4:11, Paul talks about certain specific "gifts of grace" which are "apostleship," "evangelists," "pastors" and "teachers." These gifts, given by the grace of God, are not given equally to all. They are given to specific individuals and only at God's discretion.

"When He ascended on high He led a host of captives captive." The "ascension" Paul speaks about here can be none other than the ascension witnessed by the apostles after the resurrection. Read Luke 9:51: "And it came about, when the days were approaching for **His ascension**, that He was determined to go to Jerusalem" and Luke 24:50-51: "And He led them (the apostles) out as far as Bethany, and He lifted up His hands and blessed them. While He was blessing them, He parted from them and was **carried up** into heaven."

The "host of captives" that Jesus led "captive" when He ascended are all of those people Jesus took with Him (figuratively) into heaven as He ascended. They had been "captives" of Satan and were in bondage (slavery) to sin. Consequently, they were doomed to eternal punishment, but through faith in Jesus and *obedience* to the gospel, they have become "captives" (slaves of righteousness) of Jesus and are now "doomed" to everlasting life. See Romans 6:16: "Do you not know that when you present yourselves to someone [as] **slaves** for obedience, you are **slaves** of the one whom you *obey*, either of sin resulting in death, or of *obedience* resulting in righteousness?"

In verses 9-10 Paul seems to get lost in his own analogies. He

CHAPTER 4

wants to verify his teaching about "gifts" by quoting this passage from Psalm 68. But the quotation also presents a rather vague and difficult suggestion that he feels needs some explication, which takes him further from his subject.

For instance, what is this business about Jesus "ascending and descending?" We can solve the "ascending" part relatively easily because of Luke's account of Jesus' ascension into heaven after His resurrection in Luke 4:50 and in Acts 1:9: "After He had said these things, He was lifted up while they were looking on, and a cloud received Him out of their sight."

But what about the "descending into the lower parts of the earth," part? If it wasn't for the "lower parts" aspect, Paul might simply mean that for Jesus to "ascend" **from** the earth, He had to first "descend" (from heaven) **to** the earth, but that doesn't help to explain the "lower parts" problem. What are the "lower parts" of the earth?

Although a detailed discussion of this idea is too lengthy for my purposes, I would call your attention to the fact that throughout the Old Testament the word *pitt*—translated *Sheol* in some versions—was used to refer to where people went when they died. The "Pitt," "Sheol" was down, and was generally thought to be in some sub strata of the earth. Perhaps Paul uses this phrase because it would speak graphically to those who were familiar with this concept. Following are several passages that refer to this idea.

- Job 7:9: "When a cloud vanishes, it is gone, So he who **goes down** to Sheol does not come up.
- Job 14:13: "'Oh that You would hide me in Sheol, That You would conceal me until Your wrath returns to You, That You would set a limit for me and remember me!'"
- Job 17:13: "'If I look for Sheol as my home, I make my bed **in the darkness;**'"

- Job 17:16: "'Will it **go down** with me to Sheol? Shall we together go **down** into the dust?'"
- Job 21:13: "'They spend their days in prosperity, and suddenly they **go down** to Sheol.'"

Another idea, closely associated with the last one, has to do with where Jesus went during the time that His body was in the tomb of Joseph of Arimathea. In 1 Peter 3:18-20 Peter says, "For Christ also died for sins once for all, the just for the unjust, so that He might bring us to God, having been put to death in the flesh, but made alive in the spirit; in which also *He went* and made proclamation to *the spirits now in prison*, who once were disobedient, when the patience of God kept waiting in the days of Noah, during the construction of the ark, in which a few, that is, eight persons, were brought safely through the water."

It seems obvious to me that this does not solve the textual problem at hand. Jesus certainly did not go in "spirit" to the Hadean world to proclaim a message to a specific group of people (those who refused to obey Noah's preaching). After all, He certainly didn't preach to them about changing their lives so they wouldn't go to hell; they were already there. He certainly didn't preach to them seeking a response that would save them; they had already refused that message and they couldn't "respond" if they wanted too.

The best and simplest explanation of Peter's words is found in 1 Peter 1:10-11: "As to this salvation, *the prophets who prophesied of the grace that would come to you* made careful searches and inquiries, seeking to know what person or time the *Spirit of Christ within them* was indicating as He predicted the sufferings of Christ and the glories to follow." Jesus preached to those who disobeyed Noah through His spirit who was in Noah.

Peter says that Jesus was "put to death in the body." Everyone who has heard of the crucifixion knows about that. But he adds that Jesus was "made alive in the spirit." The NIV does us a great

CHAPTER 4

disservice by translating the passage "**by** the Spirit," which is more of an *interpolation* rather than a *translation*. The NASB and NRSV, as well as other more "literal" translations, render it "made alive **in** the spirit." They say "in" rather than "by" and use a small "s" on "spirit"—(which indicates the human spirit)—rather than the "Holy Spirit"—capital "S." The NIV capitalizes the "S" which indicates the Holy Spirit, but there is no textual indication that the Holy Spirit is intended. If you feel the need, please see my lengthy notes on this topic at the end of this chapter.

Questions Over Ephesians 4:7-10

1. How does Christ "measure out" grace?
2. What captives did Jesus lead captive when He ascended?
3. How many "kinds" of grace can you think of?
4. What gifts of grace does Paul mention specifically?
5. What is Paul alluding to when he talks about Jesus "ascending and descending?"

¹¹"And He gave some as apostles, and some as prophets, and some as evangelists, and some as pastors and teachers, ¹²for the equipping of the saints for the work of service, to the building up of the body of Christ; ¹³until we all attain to the unity of the faith, and of the knowledge of the Son of God, to a mature man, to the measure of the stature which belongs to the fullness of Christ. ¹⁴As a result, we are no longer to be children, tossed here and there by waves, and carried about by every wind of doctrine, by the trickery of men, by craftiness in deceitful scheming; ¹⁵but speaking the truth in love, we are to grow up in all aspects into Him, who is the head, even Christ, ¹⁶from whom the whole body, being fitted and held together by what every joint supplies,

according to the proper working of each individual part, causes the growth of the body for the building up of itself in love." (Ephesians 4:11-16)

The reason Jesus gave special "gifts" to certain "men" was to mature The Church and to insure unity of faith among God's people. We need to look closely at a similar passage with similar intent in 1 Corinthians 12:27-31 where Paul says, "Now you are Christ's body, and individually members of it. And God has appointed **in the church**, first apostles, second prophets, third teachers, then miracles, then gifts of healings, helps, administrations, [various] kinds of tongues. **All** are not apostles, are they? **All** are not prophets, are they? **All** are not teachers, are they? **All** are not [workers of] miracles, are they? **All** do not have gifts of healings, do they? **All** do not speak with tongues, do they? **All** do not interpret, do they? But earnestly desire the **greater gifts**. And I show you a still more excellent way."

Paul states emphatically that the Christians in Ephesus that they "**Are** the body of Christ!" He then proceeds to talk about how the body of Christ is structured. It is a fact that **there is a hierarchical order** of leadership in The Church by God's specific design. Generally speaking, we have largely ignored this passage. The order is apostles; prophets; (evangelists and preaching elders) teachers; (evangelists, elders, and others who have the **gift** of teaching) miracle workers; healers; (there are many kinds of healers—physical, emotional, and spiritual) helpers; (deacons) administrators—elders; and others who have administrative gifts. Notice that tongue speakers are listed last!

These are "God-appointed offices." Whatever responsibilities are attached to those offices are not man-made, but God-inspired. Although everyone has a gift or gifts, no one has all the gifts and some gifts are greater than others. However, "greater" only refers to their spiritual significance, not to their "authority."

Paul's point here is that these gifts from the Spirit are for

CHAPTER 4

the common good—not for the promotion of personal agendas, power seeking, or fulfillment. Leaders who forget that become authoritarians and lead their congregations into strife.

This list was **never intended** to be either **inclusive** or **exclusive**; it was intended to be **representative**. Obviously, there are other gifts, such as oratory, spiritual understanding, ability to make money, to have ideas—vision—faith—a helper—a fixer—a sympathizer—a caregiver—a motivator—a prayer—a burden carrier—a decision maker.

Paul points out that these gifts are not earned or deserved. They are to be accepted graciously and treated as gifts—"assigned" to us **at the Spirit's discretion** to achieve God's purposes. Men are not leaders—evangelists, song leaders, elders, deacons—because they choose to be or desire to be—they are chosen and gifted by God.

There are three critical phrases in this passage to which we need to pay close attention. First, Paul qualified the area of his interest by saying "in the church." Paul spoke directly to what God has set in place within the confines of the body of Jesus. To say that these offices were designated by God "In **The Church**" is a different thing from saying "in **the congregations**." What may be true in "The Church" may not be true in every "congregation." This is evidenced by the fact that although there were "apostles, prophets and workers of miracles" in the early **Church**, we have every reason to believe that they were not in every **congregation**.

Second, "God has appointed"—God has "set in place" these offices, positions of service, job descriptions, or designations of responsibility as part of the divine plan of order and therefore germane to unity within The Church.

Third, "first of all." Paul listed these offices in terms of importance, influence, and spiritual responsibility. That idea gains credibility from Paul's later use of the term, "greater gifts."

These "gifts" were not given to call attention to those who

had them; they were set in place to "equip the saints for works of service." We also know that they were to "last," **until** The Church arrives at "unity of faith"—the "knowledge of the Son of God"—and "maturity." This seems to coincide with the idea that Paul expressed in 1 Corinthians 13:10, where he said, "but when the **perfect** comes, the **partial** will be done away."

Are we to assume that these gifts of office are still in existence? Tough question—especially as it relates to apostles, because it would seem that whatever would be true of one gift would be true of the rest. My response is based on my conclusion that it is rather obvious that there are no apostles, prophets, or healers (in the supernaturally gifted sense) still in existence. This would mean that the other "gifts"—"offices" may have also disappeared—but let me hasten to add this qualifying statement—"in the sense that Paul intends here."

I am firmly convinced that God has continued to "gift" people through the Holy Spirit to accomplish His purposes on earth and He also "appoints" or "calls" people to various works in His Church. I am only saying that it appears blatantly obvious that He does that differently—by which I mean "less spectacularly, though no less miraculously"—now than He did then. I would add that the completion of the "written revelation" and the vesting of all final authority in Scripture and not in people has much to do with that change.

Finally, please don't overlook that there is a "more excellent way." Relationships in the Church based on giftedness are doomed to lead to conflict. I mean that relationships between members of a congregation based on position, such as elder/member, deacon/elder, preacher/elder, or member are based on a material and institutional premise. Relationships based on "brother and sister" and the divine definition of love in 1 Corinthians 13 are based spiritually, and that is "the more excellent way."

Unity of faith is *based on* maturity, and maturity is based

CHAPTER 4

on "growing up in Christ in every way." But **unity of faith** is not easy to define. We all subscribe to the principle of unity of faith. The problem is that we cannot agree on what the specifics of faith are. It is a fact that what is a matter of faith to one person is sometimes a matter of opinion to another. Even within the confines of specific segments of Christendom, there are innumerable problems over issues like this.

For example, within the bounds of the Restoration Movement, there have been issues over the use of multiple containers for the fruit of the vine in the Lord's Supper; issues over having Sunday School classes; whether or not there is a millennial reign; whether or not two congregations could pool their financial resources to support a work which neither could do separately; the "authority" of elders and evangelists; whether or not it was scriptural to use instrumental music in worship services; whether or not it was scriptural to take up weapons in war; what is the proper role of women in Christian assemblies; whether or not the Lord's Supper has to be observed every Sunday and exclusively on Sunday; the role of grace versus works in salvation; the work of the Holy Spirit in conversion and His personal indwelling; under what conditions a person could get a scriptural divorce and could a divorced person remarry or serve in any official position in the congregation; and whether or not baptism is essential to salvation.

Often, Christians haven't divided so much over the issues themselves, as they divided over the personal charisma and powers of persuasion of the men who championed them.

A good starting place in our search for what Paul means by "unity of faith" is to look closely at the Hebrew's classic definition of faith. Hebrews 11:1 is translated in the NASB, "Now faith is the assurance of [things] hoped for, the conviction of things not seen." The word *substance* as used by the NKJV is perhaps more graphic than the "assurance" of the NASB, in the sense that "substance" carries with it the idea of "basic ingredient" or "ultimate foundation."

I understand that a molecule is the smallest amount you can have of a substance and still have that substance. For instance, the smallest amount of water you can have is a molecule—made up of two parts hydrogen and one part oxygen. When that molecule is broken down into either hydrogen or oxygen, you no longer have water. When the Christian System—composed of doctrines, traditions, customs, and opinions—breaks down and only one molecule is left, that molecule is faith. **Faith** is what has to remain for Christianity to exist.

In Jude 3, Jude exhorts his audience to "contend earnestly for **the** faith which was once for all delivered to the Saints." What is "**the** faith?" Whatever it is, I believe that we can be assured that it is the same as the "one faith" of Ephesians 4:3. If Paul's "one faith" includes a perfect understanding of **all** of the possible doctrinal positions that can be held, then no one has ever had that "one faith." However, if Paul's "one faith" contains **no** doctrinal concepts, the whole concept of faith becomes relative, personal, subjective, and ultimately meaningless.

So what is the bedrock of our faith? Deciding what Christians *have to agree on* to be united in Jesus has proven to be an impossible and sometimes volatile task. What seems relatively unimportant to people may be of great consequence to God. For instance, one small bite of a piece of fruit would seem terribly inconsequential to us, but to God it changed the history of the world. Uzza touching the Ark of the Covenant out of concern for its safety seems commendable to us, but God struck him dead for his irreverence. Nadab and Abihu using fire from the wrong place to light the sacrificial fire seems a rather innocuous transgression to us, but to God it was reprehensible. Ananias and Sapphira giving part of the sale of their house and saying they gave it all might seem a small thing to us but it cost them their lives.

We do have a place to begin however. The first and great commandment has never changed. Matthew records in 22:34-40, "Hearing that Jesus had silenced the Sadducees, the Pharisees

CHAPTER 4

got together. One of them, an expert in the law, tested him with this question: 'Teacher, which is the greatest commandment in the Law?' Jesus replied: 'Love the Lord your God with all your heart and with all your soul and with all your mind.' This is the **first** and **greatest** commandment. And the second is like it: 'Love your neighbor as yourself.' **All the Law and the Prophets hang on these two commandments'"** (NIV).

We can have absolute faith in the unchanging fact that loving God and loving our fellow man has always been and always will be the foundation of our relationship with God. All other commandments have to be understood in the light of these two. No other commandment can be interpreted in such a way that it contradicts either of them.

There are some other teachings that are of foundational importance. They are what I choose to call "salvation" or "sonship" teachings. Paul writes in Galatians 1:6-8, "I am amazed that you are so quickly deserting Him who called you by the grace of Christ, for a different gospel; which is [really] not another; only there are some who are disturbing you, and want to distort the gospel of Christ. But even if we, or an angel from heaven, should preach to you a gospel contrary to what we have preached to you, he is to be accursed."

So what is a "different gospel"? It is any gospel that takes the focus off the divinity and supremacy of Christ and the message of the cross. It is any gospel that does not include everything that God has stated as being necessary to salvation. Please look closely at all of the following passages and take note of what the apostles emphasized as they proclaimed the gospel.

In Acts 2:38, on the day of Pentecost, when the full gospel was first proclaimed by the inspiration of the Holy Spirit, what did Peter preach and insist upon? First, that Jesus, whom they had crucified, be accepted as God's Messiah, as Lord and Christ. Second, that they "Repent and be baptized."

What did Phillip preach to the Eunuch in Acts 8:34-36? "The eunuch asked Philip, 'Tell me, please, who is the prophet talking about, himself or someone else?' Then Philip began with that very passage of Scripture and told him **the good news about Jesus**. As they traveled along the road, they came to some water and the eunuch said, 'Look, here is water. What can stand in the way of my being baptized?'" (NIV)

The preaching of Jesus—because the gospel is more than just the "good news" of the death, burial, and resurrection of Christ—conveys a "right response" to that good news. What did Peter preach to Cornelius in Acts 10:42-43? "And He ordered us to preach to the people, and solemnly to testify that this (Jesus) is the one who has been appointed by God as judge of the living and the dead. Of Him all the prophets bear witness that through His name **everyone who believes in Him** receives forgiveness of sins."

Peter said that God accepts those who fear Him and **do right**. He based the credibility of his message on the fact that "Jesus is *Lord* of all"—that He was crucified, and that God raised Him from the dead. Jesus is also *judge* of all, and "Everyone who believes in Him receives forgiveness." When Paul spoke of "unity of faith" these are the things he spoke of.

In Acts 17:30, what did Paul preach to the people of Athens? "Therefore having overlooked the times of ignorance, God is now declaring to men that all people everywhere should **repent**."

Note these additional verses:

- 1 Corinthians 15:3-5: "For what I received I passed on to you as of **first importance**: that **Christ died** for our sins according to the Scriptures, that he was buried, that **he was raised** on the third day according to the Scriptures, and that he appeared to Cephas, and then to the Twelve" (NIV).
- Acts 24:24-25: "But some days later Felix arrived with

CHAPTER 4

Drusilla, his wife who was a Jewess, and he sent for Paul and heard him speak about faith in Christ Jesus. But as he was discussing **righteousness, self-control** and **the judgment** to come, Felix became frightened and said, 'Go away for the present, and when I find time I will summon you.'"

Don't forget what we studied earlier in this book:, "For **by grace** you have been saved **through faith**; and that not of yourselves, [it is] the gift of God; not as a result of works, that no one may boast" (Ephesians 2:8-9).

The seven "ones" we have just reviewed are foundational to the gospel and to salvation. We will not be mature, equipped for the work of ministry, or united in faith and the knowledge of the Son of God until we are firmly rooted in these **facts**. We will continue to be tossed about by every wind of doctrine until we put our feet firmly on the rock of Scripture, taking it at face value whenever possible and building our faith on what is clear, plain, and repeated, rather than the obscure.

Paul seems to have these four concerns for the Christians in Ephesus. First, he was concerned that they not be "tossed here and there and carried about by every wind of doctrine..." (Ephesians 4:14). That means that there must be some concrete, unchanging, immutable, and non-negotiable truths and convictions in their faith. Second, he implored that they "speak the truth **in love**." It is possible to speak the truth in an unloving way. It is also possible to speak in a loving way and not speak the truth. Third, he wanted them to "**grow up** in every way into Him who is the head, into Christ." Fourth, he longed for the entire congregation to work toward **common goals**, with each member doing his part.

Paul concluded this section by referring to how a mature body of believers is supposed to work together. Whatever "gift" God has given to each member is to be used for the common good. It is not to be utilized for the personal aggrandizement and welfare of the individual. Every person is supposed to understand his gift and his role.

Questions Over Ephesians 4:11-16

1. What was God's purpose in giving special "gifts" to certain men? Do you think He gave "gifts" to women as well?
2. How would those gifts accomplish that purpose?
3. What is the difference between saying "in the church" and saying "in the congregations?"
4. What does it mean to "equip the saints for works of service?"
5. Are we to assume that these "offices," "gifts," and talents are still in existence? Why or why not? If not, what has replaced them?
6. Why is unity of faith so hard to achieve?
7. Make a list of all of the things Christians have to agree on to have unity of faith, and discuss each one.
8. What is the "more excellent way?"
9. In Galatians 1:6-9 Paul refers to those who proclaim "a different gospel." If it isn't a different gospel, what is it?
10. What did Paul preach that was of "first importance?" What does "first importance mean?"
11. What four concerns does Paul have for the Christians in Ephesus?

[17]"So this I say, and affirm together with the Lord, that you walk no longer just as the Gentiles also walk, in the futility of their mind, [18]being darkened in their understanding, excluded from the life of God because of the ignorance that is in them, because of the hardness of their heart; [19]and they, having become callous, have given themselves over to sensuality for the practice of every kind of impurity with greediness. [20]But you did not learn

CHAPTER 4

Christ in this way, ²¹if indeed you have heard Him and have been taught in Him, just as truth is in Jesus, ²²that, in reference to your former manner of life, you lay aside the old self, which is being corrupted in accordance with the lusts of deceit, ²³and that you be renewed in the spirit of your mind, ²⁴and put on the new self, which in the likeness of God has been created in righteousness and holiness of the truth."
(Ephesians 4: 17-24)

We see some "apostolic authority" asserted by the apostle Paul when he insisted that the Ephesians "no longer walk just as the Gentiles also walk, in the futility of their mind." I believe that those who accept leadership responsibilities in God's congregations today have the same responsibility and authority to insist on Christ-like behavior among God's people.

The basis for Paul's insistence is "in the Lord." This has two meanings. First, neither Paul nor we has any "authority" over those who are "outside of the body." As Paul wrote in 1 Corinthians 5:9-13, "I wrote you in my letter not to associate with immoral people; I *did not at all mean* with the immoral people of this world, or with the covetous and swindlers, or with idolaters, for then you would have to go out of the world. But actually, I wrote to you not to associate with any *so-called brother* if he is an immoral person, or covetous, or an idolater, or a reviler, or a drunkard, or a swindler—not even to eat with such a one. For what have I to do with *judging outsiders*? Do you not judge *those who are within the church*? But those who are outside, God judges. Remove the wicked man *from among yourselves*."

Second, the basis of Paul's insistence is their common allegiance to Jesus. When we confess our faith in Jesus and submit our lives to Him, we voluntarily place ourselves under not only "His" authority, but under the authority of His Word—the Scriptures. If we refuse to live by the dictates of Scripture, we rebel against Jesus Himself. We must remember that it is not some person's interpretation of Scripture, or even our own interpretation, to which we are in submission, but to Scripture itself and the absolute Lordship of Jesus.

What is "futile" about Gentile thinking? The Gentile world believed—as do most people today—that this life—this material world—is all there is. They believed that since you "only go around once," the highest good that a person can achieve in life is in personal happiness. Even doing good things, as well as being benevolent and kind to others, is done strictly for the personal happiness it brings. That kind of thinking leads to futility because happiness becomes the by-product of *what you do*, rather than *who you are*; therefore, it is never permanent. Futile thinking leads people to live like dogs—only for the moment—and die like dogs.

The intellectual Gentiles thought that reason, philosophy, intellectual investigation, and science would ultimately provide the answers to all of their questions about the meaning and purpose of life. Modern "Gentiles" believe that the human wisdom found in science, psychology, new age thinking, archaeology, and technology will eventually answer all of those questions. This is futile thinking because it is totally dependent upon tragically flawed, mortal people finding perfect answers to the meaning and purpose of life.

Verses 18-19 give us further descriptions of these Gentiles, "They are darkened in their understanding and separated from the life of God because of the ignorance that is in them due to the hardening of their hearts. Having lost all sensitivity, they have given themselves over to **sensuality** so as to indulge in every kind of impurity, and they are full of greed" (NIV).

Christianity is a *holistic* approach to life. It is designed to change not just the way we live, but the way we **think**. It alters the way we define what is good, just, moral, right and wrong. Christianity teaches us to love others in the divine sense—not in the material sense. It changes the way we choose friends, spend

CHAPTER 4

our time, decide what we listen to, what we watch and how we make decisions. Paul's exhorts these Christians in Ephesus—many of whom are "Gentiles" by birth and definition—(perhaps "pagan" would better translate Paul's meaning) to no longer "live" as they did formerly.

He does not single out any particular aspect of human behavior for change—such as sensuality, morality, or integrity. He says that their obedience to the gospel gives him a right to expect a **total change** not only in the way they act but also in the way they approach life.

"Darkened in understanding" applies to those who have a self-centered and material foundation underlying all of their decisions about the meaning and purpose of life. Since the only "world" they acknowledge is the material world and self gratification is the only justification necessary for any action, they spend their lives in meaningless material pursuits; futility is the only possible end.

They do not discriminate or moderate in the area of sensuality. Their own satisfaction and gratification is their only concern. When the idea of God is removed from man's thoughts, only the animal passions are left. Honor, guilt, truth, integrity, and caring more about others than yourself are traits of religious fools, and the only way to silence a guilty conscience is to "drug it" into forgetfulness. The inevitable result of godlessness is that there is nothing to restrain the flesh and its animalistic appetites.

Any person who "loves the world" is cut off from the potentials of "life in the spirit" and "alienated from the life of God." To be able to live with themselves or to silence a guilty conscience, people willfully choose ignorance rather than the light of truth. They deliberately harden their hearts against any feelings of regret or remorse, and they refuse to consider the consequences that will result if they are wrong. They hope for no heaven; they fear no hell.

We are witnessing **the same tendency** in our own culture; in fact, in some ways our situation is worse. Medical science, psychology, modern "medicine," and the media have provided the means that allow people to ignore God and live like animals. We have abortion clinics, where millions of mothers go to have their babies deliberately murdered. Modern technology is used to make the curse of the vile filth that is commonly termed, *pornography* readily available even to children in triple X-rated, "adult" movies on TV and the Internet. The kinds of people who capture the entertainment headlines are all testimony to the perverted, distorted, sick, and animalistic fixations our culture has. They are evidence of the fact that we have "abandoned ourselves to licentiousness and impurity" as a result of the loss of "sensitivity."

Note that they have "lost" sensitivity. That means that they had it because they were made in God's image. They have suppressed and defeated those higher inclinations for so long that they no longer feel pangs of conscience, guilt, or regret. Paul's words in Romans 1:18-25 that describe the moral depravity of first-century culture could just as easily have been written today.

The gross hypocrisy and inanity of our government in censoring the advertisement and sale of tobacco products is beyond belief. (I'm glad they did.) Consider this: California and other states have succeeded in making marijuana legal (for medicinal purposes—what a joke) and banned cigarettes. Tobacco ads are being replaced with beer commercials. Alcohol has done far more damage to our culture and costs far more in health costs and work loss, not to mention what it costs in unwed mothers, divorce, drug addiction, robbery, rape, crime of every description, the loss of our youth, traffic deaths, etc. than tobacco ever dreamed of doing.

Let's review the words of Ephesians 4:20-24: "But you did not learn Christ in this way, if indeed you have heard Him and have been taught in Him, just as truth is in Jesus, that, in reference to your former manner of life, you lay aside the old self, which is being corrupted in accordance with the lusts of deceit, and that you be renewed in the spirit of your mind, and put on the new self, which in *the likeness of* God has been created in righteousness and holiness of the truth."

The Christians in Ephesus were taught that accepting Jesus meant that they had to change by putting to death the old self—the person controlled by fleshly passions and materialistic thinking—so that a new, transformed life could emerge. That is Paul's point in Romans 6:3-4, "Or do you not know that all of us who have been baptized into Christ Jesus have been baptized into His death? Therefore we have been buried with Him through baptism into death, so that as Christ was raised from the dead through the glory of the Father, so we too might walk in newness of life."

Why does Paul say that human desires are deceitful? What we desire always **looks better** than it really is. Think about Eve and the fruit. The illusions that Satan presents to us in this material world are just exactly that, "illusions." They can never deliver what they promise. Fleshly desires promise satisfaction and contentment but create frustration and an insatiable craving that drives us on a quest for more. Solomon said that those who "love money will never have enough money." That same thing is true with everything in this world, whether cars, clothes, sex, money, food, houses, power, athletic equipment, or the latest electronic gadgets.

Gratifying our material lusts by buying things promises fulfillment, but it delivers "dissatisfaction." Gratification promises peace, but it delivers chaos and guilt. It promises happiness and delivers depression and pain. Desire creates an illusion that reality can never live up to. And so we go on searching in a vain pursuit for what was never there.

Questions Over Ephesians 4:17-24

1. What "apostolic authority" does Paul have to insist that the Ephesians "no longer live as the Gentiles do?"
2. How did the Gentiles live? Are there any similarities between them and our culture today?
3. Why does Paul say that he insists on "in the Lord?"
4. What is futile about Gentile thinking?
5. What does it mean to say that Christianity is a holistic approach to life?
6. When the idea of God is removed from man's thoughts, what is the result?
7. How is the idea of God being removed from our culture?
8. What happens in baptism that empowers us to "live a new life?"
9. Why are fleshly desires deceitful?

^{25}"Therefore, laying aside falsehood, speak truth each one [of you,] with his neighbor, for we are members of one another. ^{26}Be angry and [yet] do not sin; do not let the sun go down on your anger, ^{27}and do not give the devil an opportunity. ^{28}He who steals must steal no longer; but rather he must labor, performing with his own hands what is good, so that he will have [something] to share with one who has need. ^{29}Let no unwholesome word proceed from your mouth, but only such [a word] as is good for edification according to the need [of the moment,] so that it will give grace to those who hear. ^{30}Do not grieve the Holy Spirit of God, by whom you were sealed for the day of redemption. ^{31}Let all bitterness and wrath and anger and clamor and slander be put away from you, along with all malice. ^{32}Be kind to one another,

CHAPTER 4

tender-hearted, forgiving each other, just as God in Christ also has forgiven you.
(Ephesians 4:25-32)

"Therefore"—always watch the "therefores." It means, "Based on what I just said, the following things are true." You'll need to look back at what he just said to understand what he is about to say. Paul proceeded to give a series of practical admonitions based on his expectation that the Christians in Ephesus had accepted the truth of what he had just affirmed—that professing faith in Jesus places great restrictions on their behavior—not only in what it forbids—but in what it demands.

I think it would be helpful for us to look at some statements from a similar passage in Colossians 3:1, which contains the same themes. "Therefore if then you have been raised up with Christ, **keep seeking the things above**, where Christ is, seated at the right hand of God. Set your mind on the things above, not on the things that are on earth. For **you have died** and **your life is hidden with Christ in God**. When Christ, who is our life, is revealed, then you also will be revealed with Him in glory. Therefore consider the members of your earthly body as dead to immorality, impurity, passion, evil desire, and greed, which amounts to idolatry. For it is because of these things that the wrath of God will come upon the sons of disobedience, and in them you also once walked. But now you also, put them all aside: anger, wrath, malice, slander, [and] abusive speech from your mouth. Do not lie to one another, since you laid aside **the old self** with its [evil] practices, and have put on **the new self**."

Paul contrasted the way the Colossian Christians were *before Christ* with the way they are to be *after Christ*. The importance of the contrast is not only for what it means to the Christian, but to the non-Christian. Non-Christians, especially those who knew us before we became Christians, must be able to see a highly practical, observable difference, first in the way we **act**, second, in the way we **think**.

Paul's first instruction is to "set your minds on things above." That means to focus your attention on spiritual matters. Notice that our ability to do that is based on the fact that we died with Christ so that we could be "raised with Christ." The rest of Paul's instructions in this passage are based on the death, burial, and resurrection of Jesus, but **also** on the fact of the death, burial, and resurrection of those who are "in Christ."

Based on what God did in us when we were "born from above," we must "*Put to death*, whatever belongs to our earthly nature." By that he meant sexual immorality, impurity, lust, evil desires, and greed. All of these things are products of "our earthly nature"—the flesh and its desires. Every Christian must look closely and honestly at his life to determine to what extent these desires are still in control. There is only one thing that Scripture says will **empower us** to put those things to death—the indwelling Holy Spirit (Romans 8).

In Colossians 3:8, Paul listed more things we must rid from our lives. Read this list slowly: anger, wrath, malice, slander, filthy language. If we pause between these words and read them slowly enough to let them sink in, I'm sure that all of us will begin to squirm a little. Becoming a Christian does not automatically remove all of our earthly, fleshly desires and temperament. "Getting rid of" is a **process**, and a lot of conviction, self-examination, prayer, struggling, and pain is involved in that purification process.

Paul said that they must stop *lying*. That Christians must stop lying seems so obvious that we wonder why Paul would not only mention it, but also make it a separate item and draw attention to it. I would point out that the tendency toward "political correctness" (saying what is calculated to keep us from appearing to be opposing popular opinion) was just as prevalent

CHAPTER 4

2,000 years ago as it is now and it leads to lying. There is always the temptation to say or relate things in a way that will make us appear better than we are. Consider, for a moment, Ananias and Sapphira.

Unfortunately, we often prefer lies to the truth, because the truth is not what we wish it to be. That is why we stand in awe of John the Baptist when he tells King Herod to his face, "It is not lawful for you to be married to your half sister" (Mark 6:18). We feel the same way when we hear Paul say that he "withstood" Peter "to his face, before them all" (Galatians 2:11). And how we admire Jesus when he says to the Pharisees, "You are of your father the devil, for he is a liar and the father of lies" (John 8:44). People often ask me what I think about a certain book or a certain theological issue. The temptation to say something inoffensive is almost overwhelming because they only want to hear my opinion if it agrees with theirs. If it doesn't, the conversation is over—maybe even the friendship.

Paul's admonition in verses 26-27 to, "Be angry and [yet] do not sin; do not let the sun go down on your anger, and do not give the devil an opportunity," seems like a contradiction in terms. If anger has to be "put away" (Ephesians 4:31) because it is a sin, why would Paul tell us in verse 26 to be angry and not sin?

It's an interesting passage. Note that in the Colossian passage above, Paul says that they must "put anger aside." In verse one of the Ephesian passage, he says that anger must be "controlled." Since God Himself is capable of anger, (Romans 1) and since we are made "in the image of God," anger is an integral part of the human personality and is neither good nor bad **in itself**. A person who is incapable of anger is also incapable of passion, remorse, even love. Like so many aspects of our personalities, "balance and control" are the critical factors.

Having said that, I must point us to James 1:19-22, "[This] you know, my beloved brethren. But let everyone be quick to hear, slow to speak [and] **slow to anger**; for the anger of man does not achieve the righteousness of God. Therefore, putting aside all filthiness and [all] that remains of wickedness...." James says that we must be "slow to anger," but he adds that anger **can** prevent us from achieving God's righteousness. Because of that possibility, James includes anger in the filthiness and wickedness that we must "put aside."

Anger **can be** a dangerous thing. On the other hand, properly utilized and controlled, it can be a valuable motivational instrument. We must be careful about justifying our anger on the basis of the fact that Jesus was angry on more than one occasion. Jesus was always in "control" of His "emotions" and did not allow His anger to lead Him into sinful actions or words. Human beings are something less than in "perfect control" of their emotions.

Verse 28 is a case in point: "He who steals must steal no longer; but rather he must labor, performing with his own hands what is good, so that he will have [something] to share with one who has need."

It seems incongruous for Paul to *address the thieves* in the Ephesian congregation. They must have had them. This is an excellent illustration of the negative/positive balance in the nature of the teachings of Christianity. Paul not only tells them that Christianity demands that bad behavior be eliminated—that they stop stealing—it demands that they do something positive— get a job and contribute to the needs of others. The purpose of Christianity is not simply to focus on getting rid of bad behavior, but to be so focused on good behavior that there is no place for Satan to get a foothold in our lives.

Verse 29: "Let no unwholesome word proceed from your mouth, but only such [a word] as is good for edification according to the need [of the moment,] so that it will give grace to those who hear."

Again, please notice the contrast between the negative

CHAPTER 4

injunction to **stop saying** "unwholesome words" and the positive injunction to **start** using words that are "good for edification" and will "give grace" to those who are listening. There is no part of the sinful nature that is stronger than the tendency to gossip about others in a way that tends to tear down rather than encourage. The phrase, "Did you hear about?" is seldom followed by something positive. All Christians need to realize that this is a critically important part of their testimony to a life that has been changed by the gospel.

Verse 30: "Do not grieve the Holy Spirit of God, by whom you were sealed for the day of redemption."

What does the Holy Spirit have to do with all of this and how can we "grieve" Him? In Galatians 5:22-25 we read, "But the *fruit of the Spirit* is love, joy, peace, patience, kindness, goodness, faithfulness, gentleness, self-control; against such things there is no law. Now those who belong to Christ Jesus have **crucified the flesh** with its passions and desires. If we *live by the Spirit*, let us *also walk by* the Spirit."

The Holy Spirit's presence in our lives is evidenced by two things: conviction of sin (John 16:7-8) and the "fruits of the Spirit" (Galatians 5:22). That "conviction" and those "fruits" are the marks that God places on those who are His.

Note the contrast between Paul's description of those *without* the Spirit (Ephesians 4:17-19 and Galatians 5:19-21) and those *with* the Spirit (Galatians 5:22-24). It is through the *convicting work* of the Holy Spirit that we become aware of our sins—our laziness, lying, greed, immorality, stealing, slander, and anger. It is by the *power* of the indwelling Spirit that we are able to overcome and put to death those sins. If we reject His convicting work or if there is no evidence of His fruits, we grieve the Holy Spirit.

Verses 31-32: "Let all bitterness and wrath and anger and clamor and slander be put away from you, along with all malice. Be kind to one another, tender-hearted, forgiving each other, just as God in Christ also has forgiven you."

Again we see the contrast of the negative ("put away bitterness, anger and slander") and the positive ("be kind, tender hearted and forgiving") aspects of what being in relationship with God through Jesus Christ produces. It seems important to me to call specific attention to the last admonition—to forgive—"as God in Christ has forgiven you" (v. 32). How has God forgiven us? Not on the basis of what we have done to **deserve it**. Not on the basis of our **making it right**. Not on the basis of our **promise to do better**. God has forgiven us on the basis of *His* grace and *our* sincere penitence.

Questions Over Ephesians 4:25-32

1. What does the word *therefore* mean?
2. What does it mean to "set your minds on things above?"
3. How do we "Put to death, therefore, whatever belongs to your earthly nature?"
4. Why is lying such an insidious sin?
5. What is the secret to being angry without sinning? Does God—Jesus—ever get angry? Does that make it all right for us to get angry?
6. What implications does Paul's insistence that Christians not be idle and that they must work have for our welfare-driven state?
7. Discuss the balance between the negative and positive injunctions of Scripture.
8. Discuss what "Let no evil talk come out of your mouths, but only what is useful for building up" means.
9. How can we "grieve" the Holy Spirit?
10. Why must Christians constantly exhibit positive, encouraging attitudes?

CHAPTER 4

11. Why does Paul encourage us to forgive as God has forgiven us? How has God forgiven us?

Notes on Baptism In The Holy Spirit

The baptism in the Holy Spirit is a difficult and complex topic with which to deal. I normally dislike disclaimers, but will offer one anyway. I realize that I am trying to place an infinite subject in finite terms. That means that **this explanation will be flawed and incomplete.** In spite of that recognition, I believe it has value in understanding how God works.

The foundation for what follows is my conviction that in all of His plans, purposes, and dealings with us, God has what I choose to call a normal method of operation and an abnormal one. We call the abnormal method the *miraculous* or *supernatural*. The term *normal* implies, in fact necessitates, the "abnormal and the concept of natural necessitates the concept of the supernatural. What do we mean by those terms?

In the physical arena we recognize the "Normal" by referring to "Natural Laws," such as gravity, growth, chemical reactions, boiling points, and biological reproduction. We base all of our activities and plans on the predictability of those laws. When some phenomenon takes place that violates those physical laws, we say that it was "abnormal or miraculous." We recognize in those laws God's "normal" pattern of operation, and occasionally, we ask Him to break the pattern and perform a miracle for us, by either suspending or superseding His laws.

When Elijah prayed that it might not rain, and God halted for three years the natural or normal process by which rain comes, that was a miracle—an abnormality in the physical realm, because "normally" it would have rained. The flood, the fire that consumed Elijah's sacrifice, crossing of the Red Sea, the plagues in Egypt, the walls of Jericho, and countless other similar "miracles" all attest to the fact that there is a normal and an abnormal in the physical area. City walls do not normally fall down. Water does not normally or inexplicably divide itself into two parts with a dry path in between. Ax heads do not normally float.

I wish to propose that God has a "normal" method of operation in the spiritual realm as well and that He occasionally performs "spiritual miracles." When the Spirit came upon Samson, and he killed a thousand Philistines with the jawbone of a donkey, that was a "spiritual miracle" that resulted in a physical one. When the Spirit came upon King Saul and he prophesied, that was a "spiritual miracle." When Jesus appeared to Saul of Tarsus on the Damascus road, that was a "spiritual miracle" because that is not the "normal" method that God has chosen to present Himself to us.

There are numerous other instances of spiritual miracles in both old and new testaments, but we would not recognize them as such if there wasn't a pattern of operation familiar to us that we call the "normal."

This concept is of value to us as we seek to understand what Paul means in Ephesians 4 when he says that there is one baptism. It also may have merit in understanding the "gifts of the Spirit" mentioned in 1 Corinthians 12, as opposed to his "Normal" method of operation in the believer.

First, please notice that there are only five passages which make reference to the phenomenon we call the baptism in, with, or by the Holy Spirit, and they are virtually identical; actually they all reference the same phenomenon.

Chronologically, the first is in Matthew 3:11 where John the Baptist says to those who were coming to him for baptism: "As for me, I baptize you with water for repentance, but He who is coming after me is mightier than I, and I am not fit to remove His sandals; He will baptize you **with the Holy Spirit** and fire." The second is in Mark 1:8 and is simply a repeat of the Matthew passage: "I baptized you with water, but He (Jesus) will baptize you **with the Holy Spirit.**"

CHAPTER 4

The third, in Luke 3:15-16, is another repetition of the same incident: "The people were waiting expectantly and were all wondering in their hearts if John might possibly be the Christ. John answered them all, 'I baptize you with water. But one who is more powerful than I will come, the straps of whose sandals I am not worthy to untie. He will baptize you **with the Holy Spirit** and fire" (NIV).

The fourth is in John 1:33 and is basically the same as the first three: "I did not recognize Him, but He who sent me to baptize in water said to me, 'He upon whom you see the Spirit descending and remaining upon Him, this is the One who baptizes **in the Holy Spirit**.'"

Acts 1:5 is a repetition of the first four, "For John baptized with water, but you will be baptized **with the Holy Spirit**."

The same thing is true of Acts 11:16: "And I remembered the word of the Lord, how He used to say: 'John baptized with water, but you will be baptized **with the Holy Spirit**.'"

These are all of the references in Scripture to this phenomenon. We need to note these things about these passages. Because this **baptism** is never even alluded to in either the letters or the epistles, there are legitimate doubts to its applicability to the Christian community-at-large. It is sometimes argued that this failure can be attributed to the fact that all of these letters are addressed to Christians who had already experienced this baptism. However, it may reasonably be answered that they had already experienced faith, grace, baptism and penitence, yet these subjects fill the pages of these books, so why should this critically important teaching suddenly disappear from the inspired record?

It is also important to note that all of the references noted above place the baptism of the Holy Spirit in apposition to John's baptism, not to post Pentecostal, Christian baptism. This is significant because there is no reason to suppose from these passages that the baptism with the Holy Spirit is a different activity from "normal" baptism.

Notice that in these passages it is **Jesus** who will actually "perform" the baptizing, **not** the Holy Spirit, but John tells us in John 4:2 that Jesus did not baptize! This indicates that John's prophecy was not fulfilled during the life of Jesus. It was not fulfilled in John's baptism and it was not fulfilled in the baptisms performed by Jesus' disciples. The fact that Jesus was going to administer this baptism means that the Holy Spirit was the **medium**—not the agent—and that the baptism took place after Jesus' death and resurrection. See John 7:39.

Let's look closely at Acts 2:1-4: "When the day of Pentecost had come, they were all together in one place. And suddenly there came from heaven a noise like a violent, rushing wind, and it filled the whole house where they were sitting. And there appeared to them tongues as of fire distributing themselves, and they rested on each one of them. And they were all filled with the Holy Spirit and began to speak with other tongues, as the Spirit was giving them utterance."

They were "all together." First, they didn't get together in this place for the purpose of receiving the Holy Spirit. They were there because Jesus told them to wait there. They had not **prayed** to receive the Holy Spirit, nor had they **done anything** to receive the Holy Spirit. They weren't there to receive the power to speak in foreign languages. They had no clue about what was going to happen there. Their being filled with the Holy Spirit was totally the result of God's discretion and divine intervention.

Second, it is impossible to determine with certainty from the text whether the "They" included the hundred and twenty or not. Third, what came from heaven was a "noise"—not a wind—a noise that **sounded like** wind. And that noise filled the entire house where the apostles were staying. It can be said without exaggeration that they were immersed in the noise. Then the twelve—or the one hundred twenty—saw some tongues like the one in your mouth that **looked** like fire. It wasn't fire though it

CHAPTER 4

looked like fire, and those tongues were sitting on everyone in the house.

Then, **everyone** in the place where they were staying was "filled" with the Holy Spirit and began to speak in foreign languages. It is impossible to determine conclusively whether or not there was a connection between the noise and the filling with the Holy Spirit. It can be said that there is no great difference between what happened in that house and what happened in some the following incidents in the Old Testament.

- 1 Samuel 10:5-6: "Afterward you (Saul) will come to the hill of God where the Philistine garrison is; and it shall be as soon as you have come there to the city, that you will meet a group of prophets coming down from the high place with harp, tambourine, flute, and a lyre before them, and they will be prophesying. 'Then the **Spirit of the LORD will come upon you mightily**, and **you shall prophesy** with them and be **changed into another man**."

- **Numbers 11:25**: "Then the LORD came down in the cloud and spoke to him; (Moses) and He took of the Spirit who was upon him and placed [Him] (The Spirit) upon the seventy elders. And when the Spirit rested upon them, **they prophesied**. But they did not do [it] again."

Peter told the crowd that gathered around the house that what they were witnessing—everybody hearing his words in their own languages—fulfilled Joel's prophecy. The Spirit had been "poured out." It is important to note that it was Peter himself who had just been filled with the Holy Spirit, who admonished the audience that if **they** wanted to receive the Holy Spirit, they must repent and be baptized. He did *not* tell them to get it like he did!

Baptism in or with the Holy Spirit was never **commanded**; it was always **promised**. No one was ever told to be baptized with the Holy Spirit or given instructions as to how to do it. In fact, there is no indication that there is anything a person **can do** to receive it.

The significance of this point is that our relationship with God is based on the "new covenant" He has made with us. In Jeremiah 31:31-34, God says, "'Behold, days are coming,' declares the LORD, 'when I will make **a new covenant** with the house of Israel and with the house of Judah, **not like** the covenant which I made with their fathers in the day I took them by the hand to bring them out of the land of Egypt, My covenant which they broke, although I was a husband to them,' declares the LORD. 'But **this is the covenant** which I will make with the house of Israel after those days,' declares the LORD, 'I will put **My law within them**, and on their heart I will write it; and **I will be their God, and they shall be My people**. They will not teach again, each man his neighbor and each man his brother, saying, "Know the LORD," for they shall all know Me, from the least of them to the greatest of them,' declares the LORD, 'for **I will forgive their iniquity, and their sin I will remember no more.**'"

It is the nature of covenants that they contain promises from both parties and the conditions upon which those promises rest. The new covenant that God has made with His people has conditions and promises—just like the old one. First there are those things that we must do—things like believing, confessing, repenting, being baptized; giving our bodies as a living sacrifice; and developing the fruits of the Spirit. Second, are those things that God does according to His covenant promises. He will not only forgive our sins; He will blot them out. He will be our personal God—our "heavenly Father;" He will bring us hope and peace; He will extend grace; listen to our requests; grant physical and spiritual blessings; and give us the indwelling Spirit.

However we understand the baptism in, by, or with the Holy Spirit, we *must* understand that there is **nothing we can do** to receive it. It is an arbitrary act of God, performed solely according to His wisdom, power, and discretion.

CHAPTER 4

There are only two incidents in the New Testament where this event occurred. The first is on the day of Pentecost in Acts 2. The sound from heaven that "filled the house where they were sitting" is the obvious fulfillment of Jesus' promise in Acts 1:5 that they would be "baptized in the Holy Spirit, not many days from now." That this was something different from the "gift of the Holy Spirit" promised to the baptized believers in Acts 2:38-39 is evident in that the reception was not based on penitence, faith, prayer, obedience, or baptism but simply on waiting in Jerusalem. It is also evident that there was no action or activity—not even anticipation on the part of the apostles. They were totally surprised when it happened. Remember that up until this moment they were still looking for a physical kingdom (See Acts 1:6).

The second occurrence of this phenomenon is in Acts 10 at the house of the Roman Centurion, Cornelius. The reason why I am suggesting this as the same thing as Acts 2 is that in Acts 11:15, when Peter gives an account of what happened at the house of Cornelius to the leaders of the congregation in Jerusalem, he says that the Holy Spirit fell on them (Cornelius and family)... **"Just as** it had upon us **at the beginning."**

There are some remarkable similarities.

1. Cornelius was a Gentile. He knew absolutely nothing about the gospel or the Holy Spirit.
2. Since he had no knowledge of the existence of the Holy Spirit, he was not seeking Him and had done nothing to receive Him.
3. Even Peter was taken totally by surprise and was as astounded by what happened to Cornelius as he was on Pentecost when it happened to him.
4. Cornelius was as shocked by what happened as Peter was.

When Peter responded to his convicted audience's question

in Acts 2 about what they needed to do, he told them that if they would be baptized they would receive "the *gift* of the Holy Spirit." He certainly wouldn't be surprised, and neither would they, when God gave them the gift.

The gift of the Holy Spirit that Peter promised to those who repented and were baptized would certainly not have been understood by them to be the same thing as what had been prophesied by Joel and what they had witnessed in the speaking in tongues by the apostles. There is absolutely nothing in the text to indicate that even one of those three thousand who repented and were baptized in response to Peter's message and consequently received the forgiveness of their sins and the gift of the Holy Spirit were, as a result, given even one "miraculous gift."

In Joel's prophecy, the Spirit was to be "poured out" on "all flesh"—not only on those who accepted Jesus as their Savior, repented, and were baptized. All of those who heard Peter's sermon and were not penitent or baptized still received the "poured out" Holy Spirit.

Here are some possible conclusions that we can draw concerning this baptism.

1. Baptism in, with, by the Holy Spirit is the "normal" operation of God, which corresponds to the "gift" promised by Peter in Acts 2 and is given to every baptized believer. It is the "One baptism" of Ephesians 4.

2. Baptism in the Holy Spirit is a phenomenon of the first century that has nothing to do with the "one baptism" of Ephesians 4. It was enacted by God at His personal discretion on only two occasions, for two "special purposes," and we have no reason to believe that it ever did or will ever occur again.

3. Baptism in the Holy Spirit is a special, providential operation, not connected to the one baptism of Ephesians

CHAPTER 4

4. It is performed by God solely at His discretion and according to His eternal purpose, which He has chosen to perform throughout the Old Testament and in at least two cases in the New Testament, and which He may elect to perform at any time and in any place in the future that His wisdom deems necessary.

4. Baptism in the Holy Spirit, or at least the effect of that baptism, is not a separate concept from that which was imparted through the laying on of the hands of the apostles and is made available to all Christians through baptism, prayer, and personal commitment to God's will. It is synonymous with the baptism of Ephesians 4.

There are some questions we need to answer before we can make a decision about which—if any—or some combination—of these possible explanations is the correct one.

1. Is baptism in the Holy Spirit a completely separate action from baptism in water?
   Answer: In the two specific cases mentioned above, i.e. Acts 2:2 and Acts 10:44; yes, it definitely is. If it is the same as being "filled with the Spirit" in the Old Testament, it is.

2. Is baptism in the Holy Spirit different from that dispensation of the Spirit, which people received through the laying on of the apostles' hands?
   Answer: It is obviously different in how it was received. They are different in that there was no human agent involved in the baptism in the Spirit of Acts 2 and 10, and obviously there was in the laying on of hands. The "gifts" of the Spirit that were imparted through the laying on of hands and those imparted through the baptism in the Spirit are similar because they both always resulted in a demonstration of supernatural giftedness.

3. How important is that difference?

Answer: In the first instance, the baptism is received solely at God's discretion with no human agent involved and no knowledge or intention on the part of the receiver. In the second—laying on of hands—although the power is God's, there is a human agent not only in evidence, but apparently *necessary* to the reception (see Acts 8). In the second, the imparting is planned and intentional, with the receiver's approbation. In Acts 2:38, 39 those who receive the Spirit as a gift **do something** to receive Him, but there is no human agent necessary or involved.

It is worth noting that in every recorded instance when the gift of the Spirit is received as a result of being baptized, there are no external, supernatural manifestations recorded.

4. Did the apostles have some options (some power in this area) not available to others?

Answer: It would appear that they did. (See Acts 8 and 19.)

It seems rather useless and non-productive to spend a lot of time debating this topic when all of the following blessings are ours due to the indwelling of the Spirit, which we all receive when we are born from above in baptism.

1. There can be no doubt that every believer receives the *gift* of the Holy Spirit in baptism (Acts 2:38, 39).

2. There can be no doubt that the Holy Spirit *lives* in us (1 Corinthians 6:1-9 and Romans 8:9-27).

3. "Now **we have received**, not the spirit of the world, but **the Spirit who is from God**, so that we may know the things freely given to us by God, which things we also speak, not in words taught by human wisdom, but in those (words) **taught by the Spirit**, combining spiritual thoughts with spiritual words" (1 Corinthians 2:12-13).

4. "With all prayer and petition **pray at all times in the Spirit,**

and with this in view, be on the alert with all perseverance and petition for all the saints" (Ephesians 6:18).

5. "...for if you are living according to the flesh, you must die; but if **by the Spirit** you are **putting to death the deeds of the body**, you will live" (Romans 8:13).

6. "For all who are being **led by the Spirit of God**, these are sons of God" (Romans 8:14).

7. There can be no doubt that the *fruits of the Spirit* are the direct result of his presence and work within us (Galatians 5:22-26).

8. "But we should always give thanks to God for you, brethren beloved by the Lord, because God has chosen you from the beginning for salvation **through sanctification by the Spirit** and faith in the truth" (2 Thessalonians 2:13).

9. The "**love of God**" has been poured out within our hearts through the Holy Spirit who was given to us (Romans 5:5).

10. "Now may the God of hope **fill you with all joy** and **peace** in believing, so that you will **abound in hope** by the **power of the Holy Spirit**" (Romans 15:13).

* Notes on Jesus' "ascending and descending."

These notes were generated by these verses from Ephesians 4:8-10: "Therefore it says, 'When He **ascended** on high, He led captive a host of captives, and He gave gifts to men.' (Now this [expression,] 'He ascended,' what does it mean except that He also had **descended** into the lower parts of the earth? He who **descended** is Himself also He who **ascended** far above all the heavens, that He might fill all things.)"

The question is, "When did Jesus descend into the lower parts of the earth and where is that?" For information that might shed some light on those questions we turn to 1 Peter 3:18-20: "For Christ also died for sins once for all, the just for the unjust, so that He might bring us to God, having been **put to death in the flesh**, but **made alive in the spirit; in which** He also **went** and made proclamation to the **spirits now in prison** who once were disobedient, when the patience of God waited in the days of Noah, during the days of the construction of the ark, in which a few, that is, eight persons, were brought safely through the water."

Interestingly, the NIV renders 1 Peter 3:18-20 as follows: "For Christ also suffered once, the righteous for the unrighteous, to bring you to God. He was put to death in the body but made alive **by the Spirit**. After being made alive, he went and made proclamation to the imprisoned spirits to those who were disobedient long ago when God waited patiently in the days of Noah while the ark was being built. In it only a few people, eight in all, were saved through water."

The NIV renders the passage "by the Spirit" to avoid the difficulty presented by the following clause—"**through whom** also he went and preached to the spirits in prison." The use of "through whom," according to the NIV, refers to the Holy Spirit and satisfies the ambiguity surrounding this clause by pointing to the probability that the proclamation was done by the Holy Spirit through Noah.

The only problem with this is that isn't what Peter said. The passage is accurately rendered by the NASB as follows: "made alive **in** the spirit, **in** which also he went and made a proclamation to the spirits in prison." Peter says that when Jesus' body was in the tomb of Joseph of Aramithea, His "spirit" went to the Hadean world.

That is verified by Jesus' words to the thief when He was on the cross in Luke 23:43, "And He said to him, 'Truly I say to you, today you shall be with Me in Paradise.'" The Hadean world, "the unseen abode of the spirits," appears to be made up of two parts: "Hell"—where the rich man went and was in "torment" and "Paradise"—where the angels carried Lazarus to Abraham's side.

CHAPTER 4

It is significant to remember that Abraham—in Paradise—carried on **a conversation** with the rich man—in Hell.

So, does that mean that Jesus, while He was in "Paradise," made a personal proclamation to a restricted group of people who were in "Hell"? That idea presents some insurmountable difficulties. First, what would the purpose of such a proclamation have been? They had already rejected the preaching of Noah, that is why they were in Hell to begin with. Second, unless we accept the Roman Catholic invention of Purgatory, a place where sinners are gradually "purged" of their sins by horrific suffering and eventually are allowed to go to "heaven," there was no way for them to get out of Hell even if they "responded" to the proclamation. That understanding of 1 Peter leaves us with more questions than answers.

A much more probable answer, one that is in harmony with other foundational teachings of Scripture, is presented to us in 1 Peter 1:10-11, "As to this salvation, the prophets who prophesied of the grace that [would come] to you made careful searches and inquiries, seeking to know what person or time **the Spirit of Christ within them** was indicating as He predicted the sufferings of Christ and the glories to follow." This passage indicates that the *"spirit of Christ"* was speaking through the Old Testament prophets, of which Noah was one, who prophesied about the coming of the Messiah.

I have been guilty of taking a circuitous route with my preceding comments but felt it necessary. Now to return to the Ephesians 4 question about where Jesus went when He "descended" into the "lower parts of the earth. "

In Peter's Pentecostal sermon, Acts 2:27-31, he quotes a Psalm 16 passage, which reads in the NIV, "Because you will not abandon **me** to the realm of the dead, you will not let your holy one see decay."

Here is a graphic reason why we have to be careful with

translations. The most commonly used translation, the NIV, is more of an interpolation than a translation. The translators chose to omit the word *soul* from the text and use the phrase "realm of the dead" to translate the word *Hades*. Although it may have been well-intended, those were poor choices and fail miserably to carry the idea proposed by the author.

Look at the same passage in the NASB: "Because You will not **abandon my soul** to **Hades**, nor allow Your Holy One to undergo decay."

The NRSV renders the passage: "For you will not abandon my **soul** to **Hades**, or let your Holy One experience **corruption**."

You can readily see that this is not simply saying the same thing in two different ways; it is saying **two different things**. By translating the word *Hades* as *realm of the dead*, the NIV makes the sentence say the same thing twice, when actually there are two separate ideas in the passage. The "not abandoning my soul to Hades (the unseen abode of the spirits), is obviously a separate concept from His **body** "not seeing corruption." The idea suggested by the word *Hades* is a specific reference to the "unseen abode of the spirits" not the physical place in which the body lies.

Hades is the place referred to in Jude 1:6: "And angels who did not keep their own domain, but abandoned their proper abode, He has **kept in eternal bonds** under darkness for the judgment of the great day." God sent these disobedient angels to Hell, that part of the Hadean world where the rich man went.

In Luke 23:43, Jesus says to the thief hanging beside him, "Truly I say to you, today you shall be with me in **Paradise**." The intent of the passage cannot be compromised. Jesus said, "Today," which is a clear designation of **when** this would take place. The thief would be **with Jesus** "in **paradise**" that day. There can be **no question** about where the "soul" of Jesus was during the time that his body was in the tomb of Joseph of Arimathea. He tells

CHAPTER 4

us plainly that He was in **Paradise**. But where is Paradise?

Let's look at the story Jesus tells about the rich man and Lazarus in Luke 16:22-23, "Now it came about that the poor man died and he was carried away by the angels to **Abraham's bosom**; and the rich man also died and was **buried. In Hades he lifted up his eyes, being in torment**, and saw Abraham far away, and Lazarus in his bosom."

Abraham's explanation of the situation is that the rich man "received your good things and Lazarus bad things." He goes on to say that Lazarus is being "comforted" and the rich man is being "tormented." He then explains that God has made a "great chasm" between where the rich man is and where Lazarus is and no one can cross from one place to the other.

There is one more important aspect to this story. We learn that God's final judgment has not taken place because the rich man has five brothers left on earth.

Many have sought to dismiss the physical accuracy of this passage on the grounds that it is a parable and therefore not intended to be factual. If it is a parable, and I do not believe it is, there is not another like it in all of Scripture. And even if it is a parable, Jesus would not deliberately mislead us by referring to things that are not true.

The NIV again wrongly translates the passage by translating "Hades" as "Hell." The word *Hades* is a much more comprehensive term than *hell*. It may be true that indeed the rich man was in "hell," but if he was, where was Lazarus? We must remember that God's eternal judgment has not taken place yet, because the earth is still intact—the rich man has five brothers there. The clear indication of the passage is that **both** Lazarus and the rich man were in "Hades"—**the unseen abode of the spirits**—and they were **both** awaiting the judgment of God.

I would suggest that Hades is made up of "hell"—where the rich man was—and "paradise" where Lazarus was. "Paradise" is spoken of by Paul in another *ambiguous* passage in 2 Corinthians 12:2-4, "I know a man in Christ who fourteen years ago was caught up to the *third heaven*. Whether it was in the body or out of the body I do not know, God knows. And I know that this man—whether in the body or apart from the body I do not know—but God knows—was caught up to **paradise**" (NIV). He goes on to say that he heard some things there that he wasn't permitted to tell (I'm sure it's just as well, it might have been better not to tell us as much as he did.)

In the Old Testament, the concept of life after death was extremely vague. It is both strange and fascinating to me, that there are certainly more references to it, and seemingly more thought given to it in the patriarchal period than in the Mosaic. Perhaps this can best be explained by the fact that during the time of Moses the emphasis was on the physical nation and physical blessings.

The book of Job contains about as many references to the subject of life after death as the rest of the Old Testament put together. In Job, the phrase most commonly used to translate the idea is *the pit*, which is the English translation of the word *Sheol*.

Following are a few references to "the pit" from Job and Psalms. Note that the Job references nearly all refer to the "soul"—not the "body"—as that which goes into the "pit." Perhaps this is the origin of the idea contained in the Psalm 16 passage, which Peter uses as a basis to expand on in the Acts 2 passage quoted above.

- Job 33:22: "His *soul* draws near to the pit, and his life to those who bring death."
- Job 33:28: "He has redeemed my *soul* from going to the pit, and my life shall see the light."
- Psalm 28:1: "To you, O LORD, I call; My Rock, do not be deaf to me. For if you are silent to me, I will become like those who go down to the pit."

CHAPTER 4

- Psalm 30:3: "O LORD, You have brought up my soul from Sheol; You have kept me alive, that I would not go down to the pit."
- Psalm 69:15: "Do not let the floodwaters engulf me or the depths swallow me up or the pit close its mouth over me."
- Psalm 103:4: "Who redeems your life from the pit, Who crowns you with lovingkindness and compassion?"
- Proverbs 1:12: "Let us swallow them alive like Sheol even whole as those who go down to the pit."
- Ezekiel 26:20: "...then I will bring you down with those who go down to the pit, to the people of old, and I will make you dwell *in the lower parts of the earth*, like the ancient waste places, with those who go down to the pit, so that you will not be inhabited; but I will set glory in the land of the living."

This may be either a lot more than you wanted to know—or a lot less—about Jesus "descending into the lower parts of the earth." It is a challenging topic, and there is much speculation. This topic is not high on my list of "questions I want answered," and I will not be severely disappointed, if when the time comes for me to descend into the lower parts of the earth or be called up to the third heaven, I find that it is nothing at all like I imagined it. In fact I would be severely disappointed if it is.

EPHESIANS
CHAPTER 5

¹**"Therefore be imitators of God, as beloved children; ²and walk in love, just as Christ also loved you and gave Himself up for us, an offering and a sacrifice to God as a fragrant aroma."**
(Ephesians 5:1-2)

Perhaps there is no more challenging spiritual concept than the idea of "imitating God." The problem is that it seems so impractical, so unrealistic that we are tempted to move past the verse with a shrug of the shoulders and make little or no attempt to incorporate the idea as a goal for our lives. It is interesting to me that in going over all of my notes, written over a period of forty years as I have studied and taught this book, I find no comments on this passage. That indicates that I have either passed by on the other side or been so overwhelmed that I gave up in despair.

As I read it again this time, I decided that I had to make an attempt to do something with it. My first thought was, *What a noble idea, but it is hopeless.* My second was that it would be presumptuous for a fallible human like me to even attempt to imitate God. My third thought was, that even if I decided to make the attempt, I would be intimidated by the fact that my pride, materialism, lust, greed, and self-centeredness renders me absolutely powerless to imitate God.

Thinking about being powerless reminded me of some comments I made on verses like Ephesians 4:30.

1. The power of faith is not in ourselves, but in God's love for us.
2. There is transforming power in the new birth and the gift of the Holy Spirit.
3. There is power in the fact that Jesus lives in us.
4. There is power in the ability of the inspired Scriptures to speak to us.
5. There is power in God's love for us as His beloved children. God will do for us, a lot more than we do—or can do—for our children. He works powerfully within us through both the Holy Spirit and the inspired Word.

This means that God instills in me the power to initiate *the process* of imitation. Imitation of God is not accomplished because of a flash of inspiration or an impulsive reaction. It is the result of a lifelong journey of struggle, failure, heartache, victory, pain, joy, and overcoming. Remember that Paul qualifies his injunction to lead a life of love by telling us that our love must take the same direction and be of the same quality as the love of Jesus. The love of Jesus led Him to offer His life—His very self to God in humility and *obedience*. And those are the key ingredients—humility and obedience! The ancient scholars were right when they said that all sin is rooted in pride. We can defeat pride, but only through humility and obedience.

Questions Over Ephesians 5:1-2

1. Imitating God is a command just like repentance and baptism.
2. What kinds of thoughts enter your mind when you read this instruction? Are they negative or positive? Do you think about all of the things this instruction **does not** mean or what it **does** mean?
3. How does this seemingly impossible command become possible?

CHAPTER 5

³"But immorality or any impurity or greed must not even be named among you, as is proper among saints; ⁴and [there must be no] filthiness and silly talk, or coarse jesting, which are not fitting, but rather giving of thanks. ⁵For this you know with certainty, that no immoral or impure person or covetous man, who is an idolater, has an inheritance in the kingdom of Christ and God."
(Ephesians 5:3-5)

In verses 3-5 we see the practical side of what it means to imitate God. Christianity is not just an ethereal, lofty, idealistic philosophy that we sit around "discussing or thinking about" (often we might wish it were); it is an *intensely practical* lifestyle, or it is nothing at all. Christianity demands obedience and change at every level of our existence. I would ask you to revisit my comments on Ephesians 4:25-32. The Holy Spirit is saying, "This is how Christianity plays out in real life."

In those verses Paul talks specifically about not lying, not allowing anger to control us; not being lazy; being a giver not a taker; and now he adds "sexual sins" and "greed." He says that sexual sins are "not fitting." What a poignant commentary. He says that they are "out of place," like a diamond ring in a pig's snout. Sexual sins are the antithesis of God's call to purity and the death of the old man in the new birth. Sexual immorality is a sin against the very reason why God made us—to be like Him.

One of the "good things" about sexual sins is that although we may try to justify them, we are never in doubt as to whether or not we have committed them. We may be able to rationalize sins of laziness, slander, jealousy, greed, and even lies; but we can find no way of doing that with sexual sins. The memories of the names, faces, and places continue to haunt us for years afterward. In fact, they never disappear completely.

In some ways, greed is much more insidious than sexual sin, because it is harder to define. The sin of greed is much more attitudinal and spiritual than physical. Greed is much easier to defend, because it seems so "American"—so "natural." This makes it easier to rationalize and justify, easier to hide, and much easier to deceive ourselves about than sexual sins. I think we are, generally speaking, more comfortable, more able to face and come to grips with Paul's sexual sins admonition, than we are with what he has to say about greed. I seldom have to question my motives—to search my soul—to determine my sexual sins.

It is not that way with greed. I have to wrestle with greed. I have to spend time in introspection and self-examination and even then, I find myself imploring God to reveal my failures in this area. Sexual sins have physical, social, psychological, and emotional consequences that make them impossible to ignore. In "extreme cases," some sexual sins are even *socially* frowned upon—or at least lamented. That isn't the case with greed.

Greed is greatly admired by many in our culture. As the lead character in the movie, "Wall Street" says in an address to a group of stockholders, "Greed, for lack of a better word, is good. Greed is right, greed works. Greed clarifies, cuts through, and captures the essence of the evolutionary spirit. Greed, in all of its forms; greed for life, for money, for love, knowledge has marked the upward surge of mankind." Even in our congregations, we pay tribute to those who are highly motivated toward financial success, by deferring to them and seeking their counsel in matters that have nothing to do with money. I strongly suspect that Satan will use greed to send at least as many souls to hell as sexual lust, because greed is so easily justified, and not only socially acceptable, but socially lauded.

Verse 5 indicates that Paul was concerned that his teaching on these topics might be taken too lightly. To paraphrase, he says, "Just in case you might have missed my point, let me spell this out for you clearly, make no mistake—this is a **salvation issue**—a **heaven or hell issue**, God is not making a suggestion or giving

CHAPTER 5

good advice here; this is a take it or leave it matter. There is no compromise in this area, no room for **negotiation**. Sexual sins and greed will send your soul to hell as sure as sundown."

I was reading over my notes on Ephesians 5 recently and was once again startled by the seriousness and strength of Paul's attack on what we generally consider to be innocuous and normal. "There must be no filthiness and silly talk, or coarse jesting among you, which are not fitting, but rather giving of thanks. For **this you know with certainty**, that no immoral or impure person or covetous man, who is an idolater, **has an inheritance** in the kingdom of Christ and God." I know of no passage that we have a more difficult time taking *literally*, and as a result, we have watered it down to the point that it has lost all definitive meaning.

It is quite remarkable that the Holy Spirit includes filthy, silly, and coarse talk in the same category with idolatry, immorality, and impurity; and He assures us that anyone who is guilty of filthy, silly, and coarse talk will never go to heaven. I was immediately reminded of Jesus' words in Matthew 12:36-37, "But I tell you that **every careless word** that people speak, they shall **give an accounting for** it in the **day of judgment**. For **by your words** you will be **justified**, and **by your words** you will be **condemned**."

It is really hard for us to place "filthy" and "coarse" talk in the same category as "careless and silly" because we consider them much more serious. They are certainly more easily identified. It's much more difficult to pin down "careless and silly," but they are linked inseparably together in these passages. Do we really believe that these injunctions are "**salvation issues**"—**sins** that we will **give an account for** at the judgment of God on the last day? How often do we devote time to reflecting on and examining our daily conversations?

Filthy, silly, careless, and coarse talk is so much a part of our everyday life that practically speaking, the injunction seems ridiculous. I mean we are tempted to say, as a friend of mine said recently, "Paul can't possibly be serious. If I took this literally, I would have to eliminate 70 per cent of the things I say, quit texting, and totally give up Facebook." I wanted to ask, "So, what is your point?" But I didn't.

We have been *desensitized* to this sort of talk by movies, sitcoms, soap operas, and texting. The kind of talk that Paul describes as "not fitting" is proliferated on Facebook, Twitter, and other similar social media options that are a daily, moment-by-moment exercise in sexually suggestive wording, perversity, silliness, coarseness, and vulgarity. I fear that even "Christians" see and hear so much of it that their **standards** are constantly being lowered by decreased expectations.

This problem is magnified by the sheer preponderance of the words we say and hear. Modern methods of communication have greatly multiplied the number of conversations we have and exponentially increased the number of words that we speak. Solomon says a "mouthful" in Ecclesiastes 6:11, "The **more the words**, the **less the meaning**, and how does that profit anyone?" (NIV) The kinds of conversations I overhear in airports occur not because the participants have necessarily anything of importance to say, but because they are bored.

Recently I asked someone who had been talking on the phone for more than an hour about the nature of his conversation. He was able to tell me about it in less than five minutes. Talking endlessly greatly increases the odds that we will not only be guilty of "silly, foolish, careless, or meaningless" talk, it also increases the probability that we will engage in "gossip," which Scripture specifically condemns as a sin.

We would do well to heed the inspired words of the Holy Spirit through the "wise man Solomon," when he says in Ecclesiastes 5:2, "Do not be hasty in word or impulsive in thought to bring up a matter in the presence of God. For God is in heaven and you are on earth; therefore let your words be few." Again in Ecclesiastes 10:14, "Yet the **fool multiplies words**;" and Proverbs 10:19, "When there are many words, transgression is unavoidable, but he who restrains his lips is wise;" as well as Proverbs 17:27, "He who restrains his words has knowledge."

God is trying to make us aware of the fact that He takes these "not fitting" words seriously and will hold us accountable for them. They can cause us to be lost just as much as lying, greed, stealing, or sexual immorality. Sin does not become less sinful in God's sight because it is socially acceptable or because "everybody does it" or because it seems a rather innocuous offense to us. We would all do well to examine our conversations carefully to see if we are guilty.

Honestly, how many of you who might read this, take these words from God practically and seriously and at least make an attempt to live by them? Jesus Himself gives this solemn warning about words in Matthew 12:36-37, "But I tell you that every **careless word** that people speak, they shall give an accounting for it in the day of judgment. For **by your words** you will be justified, and **by your words** you will be condemned." We are further admonished in James 1:26: "If anyone thinks himself religious, and yet does not **bridle his tongue** but deceives his own heart, this man's religion is worthless."

Questions Over Ephesians 5:3-5

1. Why is greed much more insidious than sexual sin?
2. What do you consider silly, foolish talk to be? Give examples.
3. How seriously, how practically, do we take this passage?
4. Why do you suppose Christians have done a much better job of coming to grips with "obscene" and "vulgar" talk than we have with "silly?"
5. What habits do we fall into that contribute to silly talk?

6. Were you aware of the Ecclesiastes and Matthew 12 passages before you read this chapter?
7. Have you ever taken these commandments seriously enough to examine your own talking habits?
8. Did you ever think that you could lose your soul over the words you say?
9. Do you really try to **keep a tight rein on your tongue**? Did you realize that if you don't your religion is worthless?

⁶"Let no one deceive you with empty words, for because of these things the wrath of God comes upon the sons of disobedience. ⁷Therefore do not be partakers with them; ⁸for you were formerly darkness, but now you are Light in the Lord; walk as children of Light ⁹(for the fruit of the Light [consists] in all goodness and righteousness and truth), ¹⁰trying to learn what is pleasing to the Lord. ¹¹And do not participate in the unfruitful deeds of darkness, but instead even expose them; ¹²for it is disgraceful even to speak of the things which are done by them in secret. ¹³But all things become visible when they are exposed by the light, for everything that becomes visible is light. ¹⁴For this reason it says, 'Awake, sleeper, And arise from the dead, And Christ will shine on you.'"
(Ephesians 5:6-14)

Paul says that we must not allow ourselves to be deceived. How would that happen? Who is going to try to deceive us? Of course we know that Satan is the great deceiver, but we must also understand that Satan is not going to come to us in a red suit carrying a pitchfork. He is going to use *people*—even people we know and love, as well as our own weaknesses—to do his deceiving. Sometimes those who seek to deceive others are the most deceived people. The hardest type of deception to uncover is self-deception.

CHAPTER 5

One group of deceivers is those who operate on the fringes of religion. These groups prey on the emotionally unstable, the regressive personalities, and those who are biblically and spiritually uneducated and naïve. They also appeal to the "extremes" of society—the culturally deprived, the culturally elite, those who consider themselves intellectually inferior or superior and those who are looking for something new or different. All of these deceivers quote the Bible (usually out of context) and speak in language that sounds biblical to give credibility to their arguments. Having said that, it is important to remember that these people are not necessarily evil people who deliberately set out to mislead others. Many of them are sincerely deceived themselves.

An altogether different type of deception comes from evolutionists, materialists, scientific elitists, humanists, sensualists and philosophical scoffers. These people attempt to deceive others with their "knowledge." They ridicule the idea of God by pointing out glaring "contradictions" in Scripture. They play on words, "If God is all-powerful, can He create a rock larger than He can lift?" Or they ask, "If God is completely good and all-powerful then, why is there evil?" I am reminded of the question, "Have you stopped beating your wife?" I would remind you that words used in a grammatically correct but nonsensical way are still nonsensical.

Ultimately, such people believe that the only good in life is the pleasure derived from intellectual superiority and self-fulfillment. With them, truth and morality are relative and situational, which means that there are no **absolute** rules because nothing is absolutely right or wrong. Ideas like nobility, integrity, and honor are simply out-of-date, maudlin, romantic notions. There is no such thing as "meaning" or "purpose" in life. Their "religion" is themselves, and theirs is the only happiness that matters.

Unfortunately, those who have accepted these tenets often are not content to dwell in their own misery and hopelessness alone.

They feel compelled to preach their philosophy of despair to others, because they cannot stand to see them "happily deluded" by their faith in God.

Perhaps the person we need most to fear when it comes to deception is ourselves. **The worst lies we tell are the ones we tell ourselves.** Few people, if any, have an accurate self-image, and even fewer want to hear the truth about themselves. We would rather hear a pleasant, complimentary lie about ourselves, than an unpleasant truth, which leaves us not only open to deceit, but actually **asking for it**.

How are we deceived by empty words? Every one of the people or groups mentioned above deceives others by making promises that they cannot keep. Why do we believe them? Because they tell us what we want to hear. They provide a sound rationale for giving in to our base desires and doing the things we want to—even though we know we shouldn't. Their "empty words" sound really *good*, even though we may suspect that they are not entirely *right*.

1. "You only go around once in life, so reach for all the gusto you can get." It's not true you know—you "go around" at least twice.
2. "Why shouldn't you have? Do this; you **deserve** it." Anybody who knows what they really "deserve," doesn't really want it.
3. "A little of this never hurt anybody."
4. "You owe it to yourself to try this."
5. "Just try it this once."
6. "Nobody will ever know, and nobody will get hurt."
7. "If it doesn't work out, there's always tomorrow."
8. "The God I believe in wouldn't punish anyone. He wants us to be happy."

CHAPTER 5

9. "You can always change your mind."
10. "Grace will cover it."
11. "After all, what does it matter? I mean really; who cares?"

How do we know when someone is trying to deceive us? The surest defense against false teaching is a **thorough knowledge of the Bible**. A second basic rule is that the more we "like" what we hear, the more it "appeals" to us or makes sense to us. We **feel better** about ourselves. We satisfy our vanity, our sensual appetite, our desire to be an insider, and a power broker. We allow ourselves to justify what is questionable; if it makes being a Christian easier, or more culturally acceptable. Whatever makes us feel these things should make us more guarded against that kind of teaching. False teachers are like politicians; they tell us what they think we want to hear. A third rule for distinguishing deception is whether there is money involved, and it nearly always is.

Please notice that having favorite passages can tell us a lot about our willingness to focus on what we like in the Bible and can lead to deception. Favorite passages are nearly always comforting. Sometimes they're convicting or challenging, but not always.

How many of you have ever heard anybody say that either of the following passages is his or her favorite?

- "If anyone comes to Me, and does not hate his own father and mother and wife and children and brothers and sisters, yes, and even his own life, he cannot be My disciple" (Luke 14:26).
- "So then, none of you can be My disciple who does not give up all his own possessions" (Luke 14:33).

Paul tries to impress us with the seriousness of these injunctions by warning us that because of deception and consequent disobedience, "the wrath of God is coming" (Colossians 3:6). God is not playing games with us. God's wrath will not always be postponed; Paul says that it *"is* coming." It is a promise as sure as God is God. In Romans, he says that God's wrath "**is** being revealed," that is present tense; it is happening now! God displays His displeasure with sin *in this world*. He does that by providentially creating negative consequences for bad behavior, just as He did in the Old Testament. We would prefer to believe that all of the negative events of our lives are related to unfortunate *circumstances*, to bad luck or to natural laws.

God's wrath comes on a select group—the "disobedient." Their disobedience is defiance to the gospel. Paul writes, "And even if our gospel is veiled, it is veiled to those who are perishing, in whose case the **god of this world** has **blinded the minds** of the unbelieving, so that they might not see **the light of the gospel** of the glory of Christ, who is the image of God" (2 Corinthians 4:3-4).

A "veiled" gospel is a gospel not fully revealed. The "god" of this world" is the material world itself; it is the "things of this world" that John talks about in 1 John 2:15, which has become our "god" that we love and serve. I remind you again that that "god," most of the time, is the "god" of self. It is the "god of self" who blinds us to our own culpability by distorting the gospel of grace and principle and turning it into a gospel of rules and legalism.

I have known people who were so desperate to find justification for refusing to do what they knew that God wanted them to do, that they searched through the Bible until they found a "legal loophole" that allowed them to salve their consciences while deliberately violating basic spiritual principles.

To *distort* means that to change the focus. In this case the gospel that focuses on the cross, salvation by grace, and sanctification by the Holy Spirit has been distorted by a different focus on a gospel of doctrinal correctness, doctrinal deletion, theological musings, and replacing absolute biblical truth with cultural relevancy.

CHAPTER 5

The focus shifts from faith in Jesus and salvation through the cross to a social gospel that emphasizes good works. We build habitats for humanity, feed the poor, fix everyone's teeth, dispense aspirin and eye glasses, and provide daycare and "Mother's Day Out" programs because doing those things is easier than confronting people with their sins and lostness. In the process, we are made to feel good about ourselves, and others applaud our efforts; however, no one is necessarily saved.

This is another area where we are easily deceived because we begin these projects with the best of intentions. The shift takes place so gradually that we seldom notice it until it is too late to change it. I once preached for a congregation that, several years before I had come, began a "Mother's Day Out" program. That program had been so successful in attracting young families from the surrounding neighborhood to bring their children that it had been expanded into a full-scale day care and kindergarten through and second grade program. It had a director and eleven full-time staff members. It was a massive undertaking and even turned a profit.

When I inquired about the purpose for such an incredible investment of time and money, I learned that it had been begun with the intention of using it as a vehicle to interest people in the church and to teach them the gospel. After a painstaking investigation, I was able to determine that in spite of the fact that literally hundreds of children, whose parents were not members of the church, had taken advantage of the programs. Most of them had even attended various special productions, but not one of them had ever attended a service; not one single Bible study had been conducted; and not one person had been led to obey the gospel. Although the congregation had hired a director, and the director had hired full-time staff members, no one had ever been given the task—much less been hired—to accomplish the purpose for which the program had been established! This is an example of a shift in focus.

The focus of The Church has to be the proclamation the gospel of the cross—not on the **method** by which we do that. There are many wonderful programs, but they do not save people—only the gospel saves. Jesus could have completely eradicated poverty and hunger from His generation—even from all future generations—with a blink of His eye. The miracles He performed were rather small in comparison to what He could have done if He had chosen to. He refused to get caught up in a "social gospel," or to get sidetracked from His mission on earth—by simply engaging in good works. We must learn to see the world through His eyes, not as hungry, homeless, and diseased, but as lost.

(* *Please see my story "Honduras" on page 171.*)

People are not lost because they do not participate in our programs or attend our worship services, and they are not saved because they do. In 2 Thessalonians 1:7-8 Paul tells us why people are lost when he says, "When the Lord Jesus is revealed from heaven with his mighty angels in flaming fire, **dealing out retribution to those who do not know God** and on those who do not **obey the gospel** of our Lord Jesus." People are lost because they do not know God and have not obeyed the gospel.

Paul's conclusion about how the Christians in Ephesus should relate to these "disobedient people" is found in Ephesians 5:7, "Therefore do not be partakers with them." It is obvious that the "them" must be the "unbelievers"—the "disobedient." But what does it mean to "not be **partakers** with them"? *It means that we are not to place ourselves in close relationships or circumstances where unbelievers have undo influence or control over us.* We have traditionally limited this injunction to those relationships that arise from friendship, business ventures, and sports and hobby interests.

What about marriage? Traditionally we have "shied away" from that application, not because the passage says anything that

CHAPTER 5

would eliminate marriage, but because the ramifications were too far-reaching. However, I cannot think of a situation where being mismatched would be more applicable than in marriage. Paul warns sternly against it in 2 Corinthians 6:14-17, "Do not be **bound together** with unbelievers; for what **partnership** have righteousness and lawlessness, or what **fellowship** has light with darkness? Or what **harmony** has Christ with Belial, or what has a believer **in common** with an unbeliever? Or what **agreement** has the temple of God with idols? For we are the temple of the living God; just as God said, 'I will dwell in them and walk among them; and I will be their God, and they shall be My people. Therefore, **come out from their midst and be separate**,' says the Lord. 'And do not touch what is unclean; And I will welcome you.'"

What does it mean to be "mismatched"? If it means anything at all, it means an "unequal" relationship where the focus and goals are not the same—a "match" that is not a "match." Why did God specifically instruct the Israelites that when they crossed the Jordan they were not to mingle with, or more specifically, they were not to **intermarry** with the nations around them? He said it was because "their hearts would be led astray" from Him. We know that is true because they did intermarry, and their hearts were led astray.

Would this mean that it is a sin for a Christian to marry a non-Christian? If our definition of *sin* means to violate God's will for our lives, then yes, *it is a sin*. Let me hasten to add that it is not an unforgivable sin. And let me also hasten to add that we need to have a **biblical definition** of who a Christian is. I mean that "Christian" must not be confined to the narrow parameters of religious organizational preferences. We must not confuse the difference between a person who is a "believer" and one who is an "unbeliever" with the difference between two "believers" who happen to disagree on some points of Christian doctrine.

Peter writes in 1 Peter 2:9-10, "But you are a chosen race, a royal priesthood, a holy nation, a people for God's own possession, so that you may proclaim the excellencies of Him who called you out of darkness into His marvelous light; for you once were not a people, but now you are the people of God; you had not received mercy, but now you have received mercy."

Peter reminds us that Christians are to be unique—"different"— from all other people. That means that Christians must develop a specific and personal Christian identity. Christians must see themselves as "aliens and exiles" in this world. We need to ask ourselves if we feel like "aliens and strangers" or are we perfectly at home in this world?

If we are to live as "aliens and exiles" how are we to "go into all the world and preach the gospel?" (Matthew 28:19, Mark 16:15). How do we harmonize this with Paul's "becoming all things to all men" (1 Corinthians 9:22) statement? The answer lies in Jesus' statement about His disciples being "in the world, but not of the world" (John 17:16). That is what He meant when He said of His disciples, "They do not belong to the world, just as I do not belong to the world."

Paul sums up the Christian identity perfectly and beautifully in 2 Corinthians 2:14-15, "But thanks be to God, who always leads us in triumph in every place in Christ, and manifests through us the sweet aroma of the knowledge of Him. For **we are a fragrance of Christ to God among those who are being saved and among those who are perishing."**

Questions Over Ephesians 5:6-14

1. Who—what—is the great deceiver?
2. How does he deceive us?
3. Talk about three different groups of deceivers.
4. Who is the person we need to fear the most when it comes to deception?

CHAPTER 5

5. What is the surest defense against being deceived by false teachers?
6. How is God's wrath revealed?
7. What does it mean to be "mismatched" with "unbelievers?"
8. How should we define an "unbeliever?"
9. What kinds of situations would lend themselves to being "mismatched?"
10. Would marriage be one of those situations?
11. Would this mean that it is a sin for a Christian to marry a non-Christian?
12. What is a perverted, distorted gospel?
13. What is a "legal loophole?"
14. On what should the Church be focused?
15. If it is true that people are not lost because they do not participate in our programs and they are not saved if they do, what does save people?
16. What does Peter mean when he says that Christians are "aliens and exiles?"

[15]"Therefore be careful how you walk, not as unwise men, but as wise, [16]making the most of your time, because the days are evil. [17]So then do not be foolish, but understand what the will of the Lord is. [18]And do not get drunk with wine, for that is dissipation, but be filled with the Spirit, [19]speaking to one another in psalms and hymns and spiritual songs, singing and making melody with your heart to the Lord; [20]always giving thanks for all things in the name of our Lord Jesus Christ to God, even the Father;" (Ephesians 5: 15-20)

Why does Paul warn the Ephesians to "be careful" how they live? What does it mean to "live wisely" and "make the most of the time?" The ideas are tied together. It means that we should live **thoughtfully**. It means that we should *give consideration* to every word, action, and decision by looking at their potential consequences? It means that we should step back periodically and take a look at our personal life and life in our social climate, so that we can evaluate how God would have us live where we have been planted.

It also means that we should see our life as James describes it in 4:14—as "a vapor that appears for a little while and then vanishes away." The great danger in life is to live carelessly—superficially—without any consciousness of passing time and passing opportunities; without sensitivity to the **meaning** of things; to get so caught up in the 8 to 5 nuts and bolts of living that we lose sight of why we're here and what life is about. I can see my failures so clearly in this area. Days go by—weeks—months—even years, and I have no specific memories because I lived them carelessly, rather than deliberately. If I asked you what you did in 1993, how many specific things could you remember? Probably not more than three or four.

How do we "make the most of the time"? God has granted all of us a certain allotment of time on this earth, and we must accomplish all we can for Him. One of the great disappointments of my life is the amount of time and energy I have given and continue to give to meaningless tasks and the way I allow things of little or no consequence to occupy my time and thoughts.

Two aspects of my college career come back to haunt me in this regard. The first is how much time I wasted focusing on and doing things that were trivial, fruitless, even meaningless. A second and more important disappointing aspect of my early college career is how much time I spent **doing nothing**. Do you find yourself talking about the weather, news, sports, hunting, fishing, shopping, politics, the stock market, the latest tragedy—with no real purpose in mind—no spiritual application—just talking endlessly about things that have no real meaning in your

CHAPTER 5

life? Have you ever noticed that when you're watching TV or talking on Facebook or Twitter and the phone rings and someone says, "Hey, what are you doing?" Invariably, your first response is normally, "Oh, nothing!" Do you have any idea how absolutely true that is?

To many, Satan's most successful temptations are not the ones that lead us to commit "big sins"—like sexual immorality, murder, stealing, selfishness, lying, or greed, but in getting us to focus on smaller and smaller ideas. Jesus taught us that "life" is more important than "living."

Two of Jesus' most poignant life statements are, "Man shall not **live** by bread alone, but by every word that proceeds from the mouth of God" (Matthew 4:4) and "**Life** is more than food and the body more than clothing" (Luke 12:23). It seems to me that the human race has spent most of the two thousand years that have passed since He said that, trying its best to prove Him wrong. It is easy to be so distracted by the "bread" of our lives that we neglect the "bread of life."

Even as a Christian, there is a part of me that says, "I know that what Jesus said about life being **more** than food and clothing must be true, and just as soon as I get all the material goods I want, I'll start concentrating on what He meant by **more**. But that is exactly what the "rich man" thought. It is another of Satan's illusions because I can never seem to get all of the material goods that I want. And so the life that is "**more than**" remains a vague idea that never becomes reality.

Regarding Ephesians 5:16, do you think that if Jesus were here that He would still say "the days are evil?" Does that sound like a pessimistic view of this world? Do you think it's accurate? Paul sees the world he lives in as going through a particularly evil time, and he wants Christians to realize that they have only a limited amount of time to influence their mates, children, and acquaintances with the gospel. Either our personal deaths or the end of God's patience will interrupt all opportunities to do that. I suppose that I don't need to tell you that the days are **still** evil. Just listen to the news every day, or look around you.

We learn in Ephesians 5:17 that "will of the Lord" is that all men should be saved, **sanctified**, and justified—that they should come to "know God." That has always been His will and that always will be His will until Jesus returns. Jesus came to "seek and save the lost" (Luke 19:10), and that is what we must be focused on and that is how we "make the most of the time." All of these injunctions call for spiritual discernment on our part. Spiritual discernment means the ability to apply biblical principles to life—to the practical decisions we make.

The biblical warnings to be thoughtful and careful about what we watch, listen to, who we marry and associate with, what profession we choose, what our core values are, who we vote for and why, what topics we talk about, the language we use, what we give our money to, who we admire and why, must all be processed through the filter of what brings glory to God and what saves the most people.

Ephesians 5:18-20 are closely connected verses. It is altogether unfortunate that they have become the battleground for the controversy between instrumental and non-instrumental accompanied worship because of the use and interpretation of a single word—*Psallo*. I am absolutely positive that is **not** what the Holy Spirit intended when He inspired Paul to write these verses! We must be extremely careful about using passages for purposes for which they were never intended.

Entire books have been written about that word; some proving conclusively that the word includes using instrumental accompaniment to our singing and some just as vehemently and conclusively proving that it does not. In my opinion, both miss the entire point that the Holy Spirit is making.

This controversy has become an embarrassing field of conflict

CHAPTER 5

among Christians, ultimately leading to a sin more serious in consequence than either position—dividing the body of Christ. This sends a perplexing message to non-Christians. It has been suggested, and I agree, that what Paul is saying here has less to do making rules to guide the Christian community in how to do its worship exactly alike, than how Jewish and Gentile Christians, who were in almost no way alike—could become a united Christian community.

The entire thrust of the Ephesian letter was to help Jewish and Gentile Christians work out the "great mystery, hidden for ages" (3:9). Once again, read Ephesians 3:2-6: "if indeed you have heard of the stewardship of God's grace which was given to me for you; that by revelation there was made known to me **the mystery**, as I wrote before in brief. By referring to this, when you read you can understand my insight into **the mystery of Christ**, which in other generations was not made known to the sons of men, as it has **now been revealed** to His holy apostles and prophets in the Spirit; [to be specific,] that the **Gentiles are fellow heirs and fellow members of the body**, and fellow partakers of the promise in Christ Jesus through the gospel."

God "set apart" the Apostle Paul as His emissary to the Gentiles. The challenge he faced was an imposing one: to bring what had been an almost exclusive Jewish Church together with Gentile Christians. These two groups were not only different in nearly every aspect of their lives, environment and history; they were intensely hostile to one another. How was he going to not only get them to accept each other as Christians, but also be able to join together in a unified worship of God?

The Jews were convinced that before a Gentile could become a Christian, he must first become a Jew by observing the customs and traditions of Moses. On the other hand, when Gentiles were brought into the Christian community, they brought with them lots of pagan baggage, not the least of which was a grossly immoral lifestyle.

Paul addresses these issues by telling the Gentiles that they don't have to become Jews in order to become Christians and that being a Gentile doesn't make them inferior. Remember, everything in the Christian community was Jewish. Jesus was a Jew; apostles were all Jews; Scriptures were Jewish; the structure of Christian worship was Jewish; and the Jews were God's "chosen people."

These verses are just one of Paul's attempts to get both Jew and Gentile to understand what the will of the Lord is. That will is that they should "all" be filled with the **unifying work** of the Spirit; they should "all" **join together** as they "speak **to one another** in psalms and hymns and spiritual songs;" they should "all' **join together** in "singing with their hearts to the Lord;" they should "all" **join together** in "giving thanks for all things;" they should "all" **join together** in acknowledging the lordship of Jesus; they should "all" **join together** in acknowledging God as the Father of them all.

Paul uses the heady, stimulating effect of alcohol on the brain as a vehicle to describe our relationship with the Holy Spirit. He says one shouldn't get "high" on alcohol, but should get "high" on the Holy Spirit. Given our present discomfort with "emotionalism," it isn't an analogy that I would have chosen, but there is no mistaking what he says. The emotional outpouring of our hearts in song is the direct result of being filled with the Spirit. That means that there must be an **emotional quality** to being filled with the Spirit that is manifested in our singing to God. This is a difficult thing to talk about or to place in objective terms since it is "better felt than told." The negative injunction to refrain from alcoholic beverages—"Do not get drunk with wine" —is objective, but the positive exhortation is more subjective— "be filled with the Spirit *as you sing...*" Singing God's praises is supposed to produce an "emotional surge."

A person may *deliberately* experience the "feelings" generated

CHAPTER 5

by alcohol by *deliberately* drinking alcohol. But experiencing the feeling of being "Spirit-filled" when we sing psalms and hymns is much more subjective, because in some ways, we have nothing to do with it. We must not overlook the important fact that our singing is not just for our own benefit—or even just between us and God. Our singing is also supposed to be **mutually edifying**. We are to "speak to one another" as we sing. That means that the songs we sing must be mutually instructive and mutually uplifting. I find it difficult to imagine how that could be done by playing an instrument, but that doesn't mean that it is impossible.

Are Paul's words about singing intended to be **doctrinally instructive**? I honestly don't believe that Paul—or the Holy Spirit—had any doctrinal or theological considerations in mind when he penned this passage. Paul isn't giving a commandment to sing; he assumes that Christians are going to do that. He is telling them **what** to sing—Psalms, hymns, and spiritual songs—and **how** to sing. They are to sing, filled with the Spirit; speaking to one another; making music in their hearts to the Lord and giving thanks.

His words have only become "doctrinally" important because of the instrument controversy that arose centuries later. Paul says that the role of singing in worship is calculated to place us in closer contact with the Holy Spirit and that it is a medium used by the Holy Spirit to **express** and nurture **internal** spiritual longings and feelings. It would seem that his words do place an inspired stamp of approval on singing and its critical relationship to worship. Perhaps Paul's assumption of the role of singing in the assembly of the Church is the strongest argument for the practice of *a cappella* music there is. But this passage was never **intended** to be used to "prove" that instrumental music was out of place in Christian worship—because the instrument was not a consideration—although it may do that.

(* **Note:** For a detailed discussion on this topic, please see my books *A Restoration Church & Its Worship* and *A Restoration Church & Its Music*.)

Questions Over Ephesians 5:15-20

1. Why does Paul warn the Ephesians to "be careful" how they live?
2. What does it mean to "live wisely?" Would you say that you were doing that?
3. How do we "make the most of the time?"
4. How much time do you spend "doing nothing?"
5. Do you think that "the days are evil?" Why or why not?
6. What does it mean to be "filled with the Spirit" when we sing?
7. Why is it dangerous to use a passage for purposes that it was never intended to serve?
8. Are Paul's words about singing intended to be **doctrinally instructive**?
9. Do Paul's words place an inspired stamp of approval on singing and its critical relationship to worship?

[21] "and be subject to one another in the fear of Christ. [22] Wives, [be subject] to your own husbands, as to the Lord. [23] For the husband is the head of the wife, as Christ also is the head of the Church, He Himself [being] the Savior of the body. [24] But as the Church is subject to Christ, so also the wives [ought to be] to their husbands in everything. [25] Husbands, love your wives, just as Christ also loved the Church and gave Himself up for her; [26] so that He might sanctify her, having cleansed her by the washing of water with the word, [27] that He might present to Himself the Church in all her glory, having no spot or wrinkle or any such

CHAPTER 5

**thing; but that she would be holy and blameless. ²⁸So husbands ought also to love their own wives as their own bodies. He who loves his own wife loves himself; ²⁹for no one ever hated his own flesh, but nourishes and cherishes it, just as Christ also [does] the church, ³⁰because we are members of His body. ³¹For this reason a man shall leave his father and mother, and shall be joined to his wife, and the two shall become one flesh. ³²This mystery is great; but I am speaking with reference to Christ and the church. ³³Nevertheless each individual among you also is to love his own wife even as himself, and the wife must [see to it] that she respects her husband."
(Ephesians 5:21-33)**

This is a difficult, controversial passage, not because the language is vague, the translation difficult, or the ideas mystical and subjective. It is difficult and controversial because it is approached as though it contained a list of "marriage rules and regulations"—or the **absolute** do's and don'ts of marriage. If it is approached as a set of **divine principles**, that have to be applied to each individual relationship, some of the difficulties and much of the controversy is negated.

The passage is also difficult because since we don't "like it," we approach it **negatively**—with all of the "but what if's" that take place in our lives due to our carnality, self-centeredness and pride. The whole idea of submission is repugnant to the sinful nature (flesh.) The questions that the sinful nature constantly asks are "But what about **my situation**?"; "What am I supposed to do if I try to submit to and respect my husband and he doesn't nourish, cherish and love me like Jesus loves the Church?"; "What am I supposed to do when I try to love my wife as Jesus loves the Church, but she refuses to submit to or respect me—questions everything I do, refuses to accept my decisions, and demands to have her "rights?" Those are legitimate questions, and there are no quick and easy answers.

In my experience, problems like these were perfectly **predictable** in pre-marital counseling. I remember warning young couples that there were major differences in their spiritual, emotional, and personality make ups, as well as big differences between the home environments they were raised in. These differences were going to create serious problems for them if they weren't dealt with and resolved before they got married.

However, I can only remember one instance where my counsel was taken, because they both realized that their relationship was too shallow to survive. In many cases, those who came for counseling were not really interested in counseling; they were just going through the accepted pre-marital procedures. They were so "giddily happy" with each other and had such a storybook, romantically idealistic and sappy approach to their marriage that they really believed that they were going to ride off into the sunset and live happily ever after in an enchanted forest. No amount of "negative counseling" was going to stop them from proceeding. Unfortunately, many of them ended up in Jurassic Park.

In all of the troubled marriages I have counseled in more than 59 years of ministry, virtually **every marriage issue** I have encountered was the **direct result** of a failure of both husbands and wives to accept and incorporate—without reservation and at face value—the **principles** the Holy Spirit lays down here.

The key to incorporating these words into our daily lives is set forth in Romans 8:5: "For those who **live** according to the flesh have set their **minds** on what the flesh desires, (what "I" want—what makes "me" happy) but those who **live** in accordance with the Spirit have their **minds** set on what the Spirit desires (what God wants—what makes him/her happy). To set the mind on the flesh is death—the death of a relationship and the death of God's will. To set the mind on the Spirit is life and peace for both husband and wife. For this reason, the mind that is set on the flesh is hostile to God; it does not **submit** to **God's law.** (The

CHAPTER 5

divine principles laid down in these verses.) Indeed it cannot, and those who are **in the flesh** cannot please God. They also cannot please others when it requires not pleasing themselves.

The person whose **mind** is set on material values is so filled with pride and the all-consuming importance of his own happiness that he is determined to get his "rights" regardless of what happens in the marriage. This causes him to rebel against the entire principle of submission. The person whose *mind* is set on the Spirit has the **humility** to cheerfully and voluntarily submit in the relationship and find peace within himself, with his spouse, and with God.

The passage begins with a general exhortation to the Ephesian congregation to have an "**attitude** of submission" to each other—**as Christians**. Pride and self-esteem are the antithesis of the Christian spirit. Unless we incorporate this general admonition to have a **submissive attitude** toward other Christians, we will find it impossible to deal fairly with the specific admonitions that follow.

Submission does not mean that we have no convictions or that we are unwilling to stand for anything. It doesn't mean that we encourage evil or wrongdoing. Remember that Paul confronted Peter before the whole congregation when he thought Peter was in the wrong. Submission in the congregation of the Lord means that in matters of personal desires, understandings, and opinions, we are willing to "give in" for the good of the body.

The first specific admonition is to Christian wives. They are to be "subject" to their husbands—**as to the Lord**. The "as to the Lord," makes this admonition specific, exceedingly demanding, and rigorous. However, it lays an even more demanding and rigorous burden on Christian husbands. They have to live their lives in such a Christ-like way that it makes it easier for their wives to fill the role they have been assigned.

Paul goes on to specify that the husband is **head** of the wife **in**

the same way that Christ is the "head" of the Church. What does it mean to be "head"? (Of course, as every right thinking, married man knows, it means whatever his wife says it means.) Paul says that "head"—as it relates to the husband/wife relationship—means the same thing as "head" means in the Church/Christ relationship. He goes on to explain that **in the same way** that the Church is "subject" to Christ **in everything**—so wives must submit to their husbands **in everything**. Does that mean that Jesus has "absolute authority" over the Church? **Of course it does**! Does that mean that a Christian husband has "absolute authority" over his wife? **Of course it does**. What has made this statement so odious to some wives is that their husbands have no understanding of **how** Jesus administers His headship.

Jesus is not only **willing** to lay down His life for His "bride"—the Church. He has **done it**. He not only did that literally on the cross, He did it figuratively every day of His ministry life. One thing that occurs to me immediately is that if we really believed this and taught it to our children, they would tend to be more careful about whom they marry. I would also ad that it is my strong opinion that there is not nearly enough, strong parental leadership and involvement in mate selection.

One of the first questions a girl should ask herself about a potential husband is not, "Am I in love with him?" but "Is this a man to whom I can totally submit?" One of the first questions a man should ask himself about a potential wife is "Is this a woman for whom I would sacrifice my most prized personal ambitions and give my life?"

Again, it isn't that the language is unclear or difficult; the difficulty is that our pride and sinful nature rebels against anything that says that we must "humble ourselves." As our culture has placed more and more emphasis on equality in relationships, Christians have become more and more embarrassed by the biblical instructions. Since we don't want to be considered nar-

CHAPTER 5

row-minded Neanderthals, we have tried every trick of language and imagination to somehow make the text say something other than what it says.

We must remember that Paul is writing to *Christians*. And we must remember that he is telling them how marriage is **supposed** to work, how God **intended** for it to work, and how it **will** work if we do it God's way. Please note the word *work*.

There are no perfect marriages because there are no perfect people. That means that all marriages are flawed—even "Christian" marriages. All married people, even Christians, are flawed. Marriages have to be *worked at*. They demand the humility to see faults, to admit faults, to beg forgiveness for, and to change "**specific**" personal faults. I emphasize "specific" because I have never yet been involved in a marriage counseling situation where both parties didn't say, "I know I'm not perfect," which means **absolutely nothing**! I already knew that. What is almost impossible to get is a list of "specific personal failures" that have contributed to the breakdown of the marriage.

It is obvious that if either husband or wife fails to be "God-centered" in their life together, ideas like "headship," "submission," and "loving as Jesus loved" simply become manipulative tools to gain personal ends. I mean specifically that if the husband uses these passages to force his wife to do what he wants and the wife says that if he loved her like Christ loved the Church, he wouldn't ask her to do that, **God's purpose** in these instructions has been completely distorted and turned into a tool.

I first heard the term *male spiritual leadership* from F. Lagard Smith. It is not a biblical *term*, but I believe it is a biblical *concept*. There simply can be no doubt that God intended for men to be the physical, emotional, and spiritual leaders of the family, community, and Church. The biblical evidence is overwhelming and what the Bible writers seem to assume is as convicting as the specific evidence. The problem is that most men want to be spiritual and physical **dictators**, but they do not want to be spiritual examples and **leaders**. They like the authority but shirk the responsibility. If wives get the feeling that their submission means that they are inferior, it leads to resentment and often to faking submission to fulfill the biblical requirement, while constantly scheming to find ways of subverting it.

In Ephesians 5:25-33 Paul tells husbands that they are to love their wives. No word in our language has been so abused, perverted, misapplied and used manipulatively as the word *love*. We need to be thankful that Paul did not leave the instruction at that, although if we understood the word in its biblical context, it would have been enough. He says that husbands must "love" their wives in the same way as Christ loved the Church. If we sympathize with women because God has laid a heavy burden on them by telling them that they must submit to their husbands that burden seems small in comparison with the weight of responsibility laid on husbands with this commandment. Any husband, who is not totally humbled by this admonition, simply fails to understand the comprehensiveness of it.

Jesus *died* for the Church and that indicates the extent of His love, but it is equally important to see that He *lived* and continues to live for the Church. I always told myself that if circumstances arose that called upon me to physically die for my wife, I would. Of course I never really believed that was going to happen, so it was easy to believe it. But even with the best of intentions, most men—me included—would be satisfied to get this "dying obligation" out of the way in some great one-time act, even if it brought great pain and suffering.

The fact that Jesus died to Himself every day of His life for the Church places every husband under the same obligation. By that, I mean that Jesus gave Himself up *every day*. He sacrificed His will, His pleasure, His wants, and His desires for those of the Church. His death on the cross was simply the culmination

CHAPTER 5

of the death He died every day to bring life and holiness to the Church. A man who isn't sure whether or not he's ready for that kind of responsibility must either get ready or choose not to marry because that is exactly what the Bible charges men to do.

In verses 26-28 Paul speaks of the "spiritual responsibility" Jesus felt for the Church and how it applies to the husband-wife relationship. The husband is responsible for the spiritual development of his wife. How sad that the opposite is quite often the case. The admonition to love our wives "as our own body" is particularly poignant. The husband is to feel his wife's pain, fear, insecurity, longing, frustration, loneliness, emotional needs, and both her physical and spiritual temptations with the same intensity with which he feels his own.

Paul says that the biggest favor that a man can do for himself is to love his wife. He goes into detail about how the husband should "nourish, cherish" and tenderly care for his wife.

I would call your attention to the Holy Spirit's teachings in 1 Peter 3:1-8; 1 Corinthians 11; and Romans 14. I would especially encourage you to pay close attention to the general admonition that Peter gives to "all Christians" in 1 Peter 3:8, "Finally, **all** of you, be like-minded, be sympathetic, love one another, be compassionate and humble" (NIV). Unless all of these attitudinal, spiritual qualities are present in us, we are not ready to read verses 1-7.

In 1 Timothy 2: the Holy Spirit gives some specific reasons why God determined the overall man-woman relationship as He did.

1. "I want **the men** everywhere to pray, lifting up **holy hands—without** anger or disputing."
2. Likewise, [I want] women to adorn themselves with **proper clothing**, modestly and discreetly, not with braided hair and gold or pearls or costly garments, but rather by means of good works, as **is proper for** women making a claim to godliness.

3. A woman must **quietly** receive instruction with **entire** submissiveness.
4. I do not allow a woman to teach or **exercise authority** over a man, but to remain **quiet**.
    a. For it was Adam who was first created, [and] then Eve.
    b. And [it was] not Adam [who] was deceived, but the woman being deceived, fell into transgression.
5. But [women] shall be preserved through the bearing of children if they continue in faith and love and sanctity with self-restraint.

Paul's initial explanation for God's decision to make men the spiritual, emotional and physical leaders in the family and in the Church is that **Adam was formed first**. Paul assumes that the reader will know that the order of creation was no **accident**—that woman's being created second was *intentional*, because God had a **specific purpose** in mind when He created both Adam and Eve. Paul would argue that the nature of God demands a *reason* for everything He does. Whether or not we *understand* or *agree* with, or *like* His reason is another thing altogether.

Another *reason* why God made Eve second was that it was God's *specific intent* that she be subordinate to Adam. She is to keep silent *because* she was made second. The reason **why** she is to keep silent is that she fell into transgression through *deception* and Adam did not. That means that Eve believed Satan. Adam was never deceived but ate anyway. At first glance, Eve's transgression seems more understandable than Adam's. Eve was *tricked* into eating; we can all sympathize with that. Adam ate deliberately, and that seems more blatantly disobedient.

Obviously, I don't know, but I absolutely love John Milton's explanation. Adam ate the fruit because he couldn't bear to face life without Eve. John Milton certainly wasn't inspired, but his reason is godly, sublime, admirable, and beautiful—and I love it, admire it, and **choose** to believe that that is the reason. I pray that every husband who might read this feels that way about his wife.

In 1 Corinthians 11:7-9, Paul gives **three additional reasons** for God's decision in this area.

1. "Man is the *image and glory of God*; but the woman is *the glory of man.*"
2. "For man does not originate *from* woman, but woman *from* man."
3. "For indeed was man created *for* the woman's sake, but woman *for* the man's sake."

All of these reasons have to do with God's purpose in creation. The implications are disarming to us because of our cultural setting and our personal pride.

In verse 31, Paul says that marriage—becoming one flesh—the leaving of father and mother—is a "great mystery." Finally, he has said something with which everybody agrees. But after having said that it is a "mystery," he concludes the section by returning to the basic practical principles with which he began. Husbands should love their wives as themselves, and wives should respect their husbands.

(**Note:** For a more detailed discussion of this issue, please see my book *A Restoration Church; Marriage, Divorce & Remarriage.*)

Questions Over Ephesians 5:21-33

1. Why is this such a difficult passage?
2. Why has it evoked such controversy?
3. What is the difference between a divine command and a divine principle?
4. Why does pre-marital counseling often fail to achieve its objective?
5. What main human attribute keeps us from submission?

6. If submission does not mean that we have no convictions or that we are unwilling to stand for anything—if it doesn't mean that we countenance evil or wrongdoing, what does it mean?

7. What does it mean that the husband is the "head" of the wife?

8. What does it mean that Christ is the "head" of the Church?

9. What are the first questions men and women should ask themselves before deciding to marry?

10. Why do you think that strong parental involvement in mate selection has been totally lost?

11. What influence should these verses have on the children of Christians?

12. Why is it so hard to get a list of **"specific personal** failures," that have contributed to the breakdown of the marriage from husbands and wives.

13. Why is the order of creation important?

14. Why have we found it necessary to make the passage say something it doesn't say?

15. List eight reasons Paul gives for why God decided to place the woman in subjection to the man. (See 1 Timothy 2 and Romans 11.)

16. What far-reaching principle is taught in Romans 9:14-21?

17. What is involved in a husband "loving" his wife as Christ loved The Church?

CHAPTER 5

Honduras

Several years ago I went to Honduras to help construct a facility for youth workers to live in while they were there doing benevolent deeds. I had been told much about the backwardness and poverty of the country, but somehow the primitive living conditions, the abject poverty, the lack of sanitation and education didn't measure up to my expectations.

I don't believe that I am a calloused or insensitive individual, but I simply was not as adversely affected by their living conditions as the advance billing warranted. I believe that my reaction was influenced by a sense of poverty that runs deeper than physical deprivation. I randomly jotted down the following thoughts as we traveled and became acquainted in that country.

Hondurans are greedy, proud, selfish, and sexually immoral. They drink, smoke, steal, curse, gamble, lie, are drug addicted, and divorced. They are sinners. Their poverty has not changed that, and **our wealth will not change it**.

Being unbelievably rich, having every conceivable educational, technological, cultural, economic, and medical advantage has not made Americans more honest, more moral, more just, or more faithful. If anything it has made them less amenable to the teachings of Jesus; less conscious of sin; less ashamed of their pride; and less aware of a need for forgiveness or righteousness.

Christians need to give careful consideration to what their mission is in Honduras or Houston, Halifax, Hazel Park, Huntsville or any other field that God gives us to till. If we do not change the **eternal destiny** of those we serve, **we have done nothing for the kingdom of God**. In fact we may not have even done anything spiritual because that kingdom is not of this world.

Hondurans are easily converted. Their extreme poverty and lack of education motivates them to accept quite readily whatever religious philosophy is offered to them, especially if it is accompanied by **materialistic incentives**. The result is that they change religions quite readily, as newer religious arrivals, who are seeking converts to display to the folks back home, are willing to offer more inducements.

It is easy to be critical of this fickleness, until we realize that Americans operate in much the same way, except on a grander scale. A new "family life center" is sure to net any congregation some new members. If you can jazz up your services, show video clips, sing contemporary music, use phrases like unconditional love; conflict resolution; dysfunctional, culturally defined morality, situation ethics, denial, disengagement, dual submission, negotiated change, alternative lifestyles, existential anxiety, and sermon attention disorder syndrome, you can draw crowds, but you may not **lead anyone to the saving grace of Jesus Christ**.

How long has it been since anybody showed up here looking for people who emphasized more faithfulness to the Bible; was more demanding in terms of commitment, lifestyle, putting to death all forms of materialism, pride, and self-centeredness? Suffering, commitment, cross-bearing, and self-sacrifice don't **sell** in Honduras any better than it does in America.

The Church is not a philanthropic organization commissioned to **do good deeds** in the name of Jesus. We are the **Israel of God**, called by the Holy Spirit into fellowship with Jesus Christ. We are a **holy nation**, a **royal priesthood** commissioned to preach the gospel to the whole world. Doing good works along the way is incidental to that mission. Good works do not save the lost, nor do they save us. The gospel saves and only the gospel! It is perplexing to see ourselves as rediscovering the concept of salvation by grace in our congregations while we continue to attempt to save others by doing good works.

Hondurans were giving birth and dying long before we went there. They will continue to do so long after we are gone. They die at birth, as teenagers, at 3, 13, 37, 63, 78 and 90 years of

CHAPTER 5

age. They die of cancer, heart disease, leukemia, AIDS, murder, accidents—most of the ways that folks die in America. We will not change that.

Honduras is a land of great beauty and grinding poverty. The most glaring poverty is in the area of spiritual considerations. They are lost, but they are not lost **because of their living conditions**. Those conditions just make it easy to **see** that they are lost. In America we cover our lostness with prosperity, psychology, paraphernalia, poppy seed, hops, sports, shopping, gadgets, Facebook, and Twitter. Hondurans are not lost—even more lost—because they are poor or because they do not work for union wages, shop at the mall, have personal computers, run to the doctor when they stub their toes, contract the latest in venereal diseases, have support groups, email, twelve-step programs, Medicare, or personal psychologists. It is not our duty to make them happy or to make Americans out of them. The world has quite enough Americans—and too few Christians.

There are many governmental and philanthropic organizations that can and will outspend us in the area of good works. We must be careful that we do not see ourselves as amateur providences with all kinds of arrogant designs for changing people's lives to suit our notions of what's good for them. We must not use Hondurans as a type of "charitable function" to relieve the guilt we accumulate because of our vast wealth. For instance, for every twenty-five Hondurans I help, I get indulgences, which justifies a certain amount of materialism.

Much attention has been focused on Matthew 25 where Jesus equates the feeding of the hungry; the clothing of the naked; the visiting of those in prison; and the care of the sick with eternal reward or condemnation. I would point out that Jesus says that those things were done to "brothers of His," which probably indicates some restricted meaning. I would also call our attention to the sending out of the seventy who are specifically told **not** to take any gold, silver, extra clothing, or shoes, which would make it impossible for them to do anything in the way of unburdening the destitute in any practical way.

I do **not say** that the clear impetus of Matthew 25 is unworthy of our attention. I **do say** that the evangelistic mission of the Church must focus its attention on spiritual matters. I am saying that often it is far easier to dole out clothing, food, medical supplies, and capitalistic projects from our vast wealth, making ourselves no poorer and receiving the acclaim of all, than it is to confront people with their lostness and suffer the risks of alienation. It also needs to be remembered that we have learned, much to our regret, that if we attract people to our message through benevolence, those who outspend us will be more successful.

In the end, if people are not converted to Jesus and the message of the gospel, they are not converted at all.

EPHESIANS
CHAPTER 6

¹"Children, obey your parents in the Lord, for this is right. ²Honor your father and mother (which is the first commandment with a promise), ³so that it may be well with you, and that you may live long on the earth. ⁴Fathers, do not provoke your children to anger, but bring them up in the discipline and instruction of the Lord."
(Ephesians 6:1-4)

It is amazing to me that this is the only New Testament teaching on the all-important topic of raising children. If we ask ourselves why this should be true, there may be a good lesson about the nature of God's revelation in it. Let me challenge you with this thought: The Old Testament has a great deal to say about parent/child relationships. We are sometimes too quick either to ignore or even dismiss Old Testament teachings on the grounds that we live under a new law.

Perhaps we need to be reminded of what Jesus said about the Old Law in Matthew 5:17-19, "Do not think that I have come to abolish the law or the prophets; I did not come to abolish but to fulfill. For truly I say to you, **until heaven and earth pass away**, not the smallest letter or stroke shall pass from the law until all is accomplished. Whoever then annuls one of the least of these commandments, and teaches others to do the same, shall be called least in the kingdom of heaven; but **whoever keeps** and teaches them, he shall be called great in the kingdom of heaven."

Could it be that God does not repeat in the new law, what He has no intention of changing from the instructions given in the old law? We need to remember that although the *basis* of our relationship with God has changed from "command and performance" to "principle, grace, and faith," our moral, emotional, and instructional relationship has not changed. God's basic teachings about how we ought to live have not changed—because God has not changed.

New Testament teachings on marriage provide a good illustration of what I mean. Paul's instructions on marriage contain the new covenant principles for the husband/wife relationship, but the foundations underlying those principles are exclusively Old Testament. In 1 Corinthians 14:34 Paul writes, "The women are to keep silent in the churches; for they are not permitted to speak, but are to subject themselves, **just as the Law also says.**"

Apparently, God has nothing to add to what He already said in the Old Testament about parent/child relationships, so Paul simply reaffirms the Old Testament teaching.

How far does the "child" status extend? When does a "child" cease to be a child? If God had intended for there to be a specific age when a child would no longer have to obey his parents, He would have told us what age that was. We all know that the relationship changes with age, but in the absence of divine imperatives, we are left to using the spiritual discernment the Holy Spirit gave us within the parameters of individual circumstances. Parents have been facing the challenge of gradually detaching themselves from their children and making them responsible for their decisions at different ages and with varying degrees of success since the beginning of time. The time and manner of accomplishing that varies from family-to-family, child-to-child and situation-to-situation.

How far does the "obey" extend and is it modified by "in the

CHAPTER 6

Lord"? Does it restrict parental authority to those matters which might be called "spiritual"? It is obvious that "in the Lord" does not restrict parental authority to spiritual matters. That would set off a whole new legalistic debate on what is and what is not "spiritual." Paul does not use *obedience* here in some special, restricted sense. "Obey" means "obey."

There may be some validity to the idea that "in the Lord" means that children must obey their parents unless their obedience would bring them into conflict with their understanding of how God wants them to live. This would be extremely unlikely in small children, but every child reaches an age where the likelihood of this happening increases. An illustration of this might be that an 18-year-old boy wants to go into ministry, but his parents want him to be an attorney. Since they are paying for his schooling, they feel they can enforce obedience by withholding money for his education. In this case, though the boy should "honor" his parents—by listening to them and being respectful, he is not under "obligation" to obey, since he feels he is doing what God wants him to do.

"Honor your father and mother." What does it mean to honor? Honoring is *attitudinal*. It is a frame of mind that precedes specific obedience. Parents can demand and even enforce obedience at the physical level, but what Paul calls for goes far beyond that. I do not at all mean that enforcing obedience is not a critical part of parenting. Obedience is not going to happen simply because the child sees the *reasonableness* of it or decides that it makes perfectly good sense. Obedience is the first lesson that parents must teach, and until the *attitude* of obedience is instilled, teaching anything else becomes difficult at best and impossible at worst. Children can be taught obedience much earlier than they are capable of understanding honor.

It is important to see that both obedience and honor are *parental obligations* before they are child obligations. Parents must *demonstrate* obedience and honor toward God, toward authority, and toward each other, so their children can see it in action and experience it. Parents who argue loudly, fight, call each other names, and act disrespectfully to each other and other authority figures have no reason to expect their children to develop an attitude of either obedience or honor toward them.

Honoring parents is the first commandment with a *promise*. God has promised that it will "be well" with those children who honor and obey their parents and they will *live long lives*. Notice that the promise is to the children, not to the parents.

What does "be well" mean? Wellness is tied directly to obeying and honoring in two ways. A child who honors her parents is living in harmony with God's purpose for her life and as a consequence, she experiences a holistic state of spiritual, emotional, and even physical health, which results in an orderly existence of peace and joy. *That is* "well being." There is also a "blessing from God" of peace and joy on all those who live according to His ways.

Is the promise of "long life" still in effect? Does this mean that God is obligated to see that obedient, honoring children live a long time? If it is, how do we explain the deaths of children, like David's son by Bathsheba, at young ages, who to all outward appearances were either innocent or obedient to their parents? That question leads me to the conviction that the promise is generic in nature, leaving room for other circumstances? It would also seem that the promise is to the children of Christian parents. That does not mean that obedient children of non-Christian parents aren't also blessed. Anyone who lives by God's decrees, even unwittingly, will live a happier, healthier, and more productive life.

The instruction of Ephesians 6:4 has both positive and negative implications. How do we keep from provoking our children to anger when it is our duty to tell them the things

CHAPTER 6

they do not wish to hear? Some of the keys to success in this area have to do with:
1. Having a proper attitude of genuine concern and sensitivity to the child's personality
2. Choosing the right time and the right circumstances for correction
3. Using the right tone of voice
4. Choosing punishment for disobedience that is **appropriate** to the infraction

All of these things are extremely important. Parents who shout, nag, and are inconsistent and unreasonable in administering punishment generally *provoke* anger and rebellion. Parents who neglect to affirm, to compliment, to give the time, care, love, and attention that children need in circumstances other than discipline will provoke them to anger and rebellion. Parents who do not help their children with history, attend their sporting events, band and choral concerts, or other activities; parents who do not take their children fishing or camping; parents who don't sit up with their children when they are sick; parents who do not read the Bible and other books to their children and pray with them; all of these parents are *unworthy of disciplining them.*

(**Note:** For a complete discussion of these verses, please order my 6-CD set of lessons, or purchase my book *Teaching Faith To Our Children.*)

Questions Over Ephesians 6:1-4

1. Why do you think there is so little teaching in the New Testament on child raising?
2. When does a "child" cease to be a child?
3. How far does the "obey" extend and is it modified by "in the Lord?"

4. Does it restrict parental authority to those matters which might be called "spiritual?"
5. Does it mean that only children whose parents are Christians are under obligation to God obey them?
6. What does it mean to honor and how do we teach it?
7. What does "be well" mean?
8. Is the promise of "long life" still in effect?
9. Does it mean that God is obligated to see that obedient, honoring children live a long time or is the promise generic in nature, leaving room for other circumstances?
10. How do we explain the deaths of children, like David's son by Bathsheba, at young ages who to all outward appearances were either innocent or obedient to their parents?
11. How do we keep from provoking our children to anger when it is our duty to tell them the things they do not wish to hear?

⁵"Slaves, be obedient to those who are your masters according to the flesh, with fear and trembling, in the sincerity of your heart, as to Christ; ⁶not by way of eyeservice, as men-pleasers, but as slaves of Christ, doing the will of God from the heart. ⁷With good will render service, as to the Lord, and not to men, ⁸knowing that whatever good thing each one does, this he will receive back from the Lord, whether slave or free. ⁹And, masters, do the same things to them, and give up threatening, knowing that both their Master and yours is in heaven, and there is no partiality with Him."
(Ephesians 6:5-9)

It is easy to be critical of Paul for not taking a stronger stand against slavery when we are not faced with the problem. The important point to be made here is that despite much modern preaching to the contrary, Jesus and Christianity do not focus *directly* on *social issues*. When one of His listeners asks Jesus to tell his brother to

CHAPTER 6

divide the inheritance with him, Jesus refuses to get involved. When the question of paying taxes was brought to Jesus, He treats it as an unimportant issue. If you look closely at His words, it cannot be overlooked that He simply was unconcerned with either government or social issues. I believe the reason for that was that He knew that when people's hearts were changed by the gospel of the cross, all social issues would be resolved.

Jesus had the power not only to heal every sick person on earth; but He also had the power to eradicate disease and poverty! He had the power to totally change—or even do away with—the Roman government and the Jewish one as well. Obviously, He didn't do that, and we should ask ourselves why, if we are to get to the truth about these types of issues. Jesus didn't leave heaven and come to earth to heal our physical ailments, eradicate poverty, and put an end to social injustice; He could have done that from heaven and *without the cross*. He came to **save us**—and that was the only focus He had. Bringing people into a vital saving relationship with God will drastically improve their social conditions and increase social justice, but that is an **effect**, not a **cause**.

There are some critically important principles here that are easily overlooked if we focus on the slavery issue. One is the basic *principle* that underlies the slave/master relationship. That *principle* is that a slave has no "**rights**"! He "owns" nothing, even his body belongs to his master. Another *principle* is that absolute, unquestioning obedience to the master is demanded of a slave.

Paul reminds us that *all Christians are slaves*: "Or do you not know that your body is a temple of the Holy Spirit who is in you, whom you have from God, and that **you are not your own**? For you have been **bought with a price**: therefore glorify God in your body" (1 Corinthians 6:19-20). The price paid was the blood of Jesus. We need to be constantly reminded of these principles. I fear that often, modern Christians, especially in

America, think of The Church as a democracy, which makes them want to exercise their *rights*, their right to their "opinion," and their right to *vote* on spiritual matters. There is also a far-reaching principle in Paul's instructions to slaves when he tells them that if being a slave is the *circumstance* they find themselves in, then be the *best slave* that they possibly can. That principle applies to every Christian in every circumstance of their lives. The story of Joseph is a powerful example of this principle.

Questions Over Ephesians 6:5-9

1. Why doesn't Paul—God—take a stronger stand against slavery?
2. Why do you think that Jesus was unconcerned with social issues?
3. What critically important *principles* are taught in this passage?
4. Do you think of yourself as a slave?
5. What "price" did Jesus pay for us?
6. Who "owned us" before Jesus redeemed us?
7. Since we don't have physical slavery anymore in our country (outside of marriage), to what situations in our lives might these principles apply?
8. What do we learn from the story of Joseph regarding our attitude toward our circumstances?

¹⁰**"Finally, be strong in the Lord, and in the strength of His might. ¹¹Put on the full armor of God, that you will be able to stand firm against the schemes of the devil. ¹²For our struggle is not against flesh and blood, but against the rulers, against the powers, against the world forces of this darkness, against the spiritual [forces] of wickedness in the heavenly places. ¹³Therefore, take**

CHAPTER 6

up the full armor of God, so that you may be able to resist in the evil day, and having done everything, to stand firm." (Ephesians 6:10-13)

Paul encourages the Christians in Ephesus to "be strong in the Lord." He tells them that the source of their strength is in the "might" of Jesus. We often do Jesus a terrible injustice by constantly referring to Him in almost effeminate terms. The words *sweet, gentle, beautiful, lowly, humble,* even the *"Lamb of God"* analogy, although true and biblical need to be balanced with terms such as "the lion of the tribe of Judah;" the one with the sharp, two-edged sword protruding from His mouth so that with it He may smite the nations and rule them with a rod of iron; the ruler of the kings of the earth; One whose eyes are like a flame of fire; One whose face is like the sun shining in its strength; One who reproves and disciplines; One who is clothed with a robe dipped in blood, whose name is called The Word of God; One who treads the wine press of the fierce wrath of God, the Almighty; One who has a name written, "KING OF KINGS, AND LORD OF LORDS" on His robe and on His thigh; One who "wreaks vengeance of those who know not God and do not obey the gospel."

Nearly every song we sing that has a description of Jesus in it, labels Him in terms that belie weakness, not strength: "You are beautiful beyond description;" "O lamb of God, sweet Lamb of God, I love the holy Lamb of God;" "Jesus, meek and gentle." We don't sing the "Battle Hymn of The Republic" much anymore, probably because we are uncomfortable with the imagery. "Mine eyes have seen the glory of the coming of the Lord, He is trampling out the vintage where the grapes of wrath are stored, He has loosed the fateful lightening of His terrible swift sword, His truth is marching on."

My point is that if our conceptual image of the Christ is limited to the soft, sweet, and humble depictions in Scripture, and the descriptions I have given above are left out, we have a distorted, idolatrous concept of Him that is not the Christ of God. Therefore, we can have little confidence in the *"strength that He supplies."*

Having said all of that let me finish these comments by referring to a great old hymn "When My Love To Christ Grows Weak." The last line is, "Then to life I turn again, learning all the worth of pain, learning all **the might** that lies, in a full self-sacrifice." To those of you who have learned the "worth of pain," through your own suffering, I pray that if nothing else good came from your suffering, you might have a deeper appreciation for the "might," "strength," and "power" required to "volunteer" to suffer as no man has ever suffered.

Paul's description of the nature of the battle in which we are engaged allows us to understand the type of "equipment" we need to be victorious. He uses the phrase *full armor* twice, drawing attention to the fact that successful resistance requires all of God's armor. It is interesting to me that the battle instructions are to "stand firm" and to "resist." There is no indication of a responsibility to take the offensive. I believe that the major reason for that is that the outcome of the battle has already been decided. When Jesus was resurrected from the dead, Satan and all of his forces were defeated, and Jesus and the Church are already triumphant.

What is taking place in our lives is the result of the last desperate, dying throes of a raging, bitter, defeated enemy. What God calls us to do is to "stand firmly" against his last offensive, an offensive designed to take as many of God's people as possible into the flames of hell along with himself. What we need to take that firm stand is the strength and might that God supplies through the Son and the Holy Spirit.

Satan has his schemes to take us away from God. Remember that Satan played no role in creation because he has no creative power; he only has the power of twisting and perverting what

CHAPTER 6

God has already created and the power of "illusion." What that means is the battle in which we are engaged is a spiritual one, a battle for the minds of men. We fight the battle *internally* in the *decision making processes* of the will, intellect, and emotions rather than externally in the flesh, That is why we need spiritual weapons to fight against the forces Paul enumerates that are opposed to us.

Here are the questions we need to ask and answer as best we can. Who are these rulers, powers, world forces of darkness, and spiritual forces of wickedness in heavenly places? Who is the devil? Where did he come from? What are his schemes? Why is he determined to turn Christians away from God? What motivates him?

Here are the short answers. The rulers, powers, world forces of darkness, and spiritual forces of wickedness in heavenly places are simply wittingly or unwittingly the wealthy, powerful people and governing systems under the control of Satan. Satan often uses people in positions of power and wealth as vehicles of influence in the world. Transversely, God can use these same people as forces for good in the world. In most cases, these people Satan uses are unaware that they are simply pawns to be used and discarded by "other worldly forces" more powerful than they can possibly comprehend in a spiritual chess game beyond their ability to comprehend.

The devil—Satan is a "created being"—an angel created by God. He was not always "the devil" because God created nothing inherently evil. Evil was something he *chose*. As a result of his rebellion against God, God cast him out of heaven along with those angels who chose to follow him, and he became a "fallen angel;" fallen because he "fell out of God's graces" and fallen because he was cast *down* out of heaven to the earth—a lower position. I want you to know that I realize that I am talking about infinite, heavenly things in finite, earthly terms, and I am just as frustrated by the limitations of vocabulary as John the Revelator was when he attempted to describe the things he saw by saying that it was "like" something with which we are familiar.

We are not told how all of these things came about, and we would be completely unable to understand them if we had been told. However, there are hints in several places that titillate our curiosity. For instance, Jude 9 says, "But Michael the archangel, when he disputed with the devil and argued about the body of Moses, did not dare pronounce against him a railing judgment, but said, 'The Lord rebuke you!'" First, since Michael is the "archangel" it means that there is a hierarchy of angels. Second, coming to grips with the fact that he was engaged in an argument with Satan over the body of Moses is beyond our ability to conceive. Was it an argument over who was going to get it? There are times when I wish we had been told either more or less.

Another fascinating reference to "fallen angels" is in Jude 6: "And angels who did not **keep their own domain**, but abandoned their **proper abode**, He has kept in eternal bonds under darkness for the judgment of the great day." What is an angel's "domain" and what is its "proper abode"? I sincerely believe that "domain" refers to the role of ministering service that God created angels to fill. Satan and his followers decided that they wanted to occupy a place of greater prominence and authority. In doing so, they sought to elevate themselves from the "proper abode" that God had assigned to them.

Remember that it is not *us* that Satan hates, we are *nothing to him*. He seeks our destruction because God loves us, and we are therefore *something to God*. It is because he hates God so much that we become significant to him. In 1 Chronicles 21:1 we read, "Satan stood up against Israel, and *moved David* to number Israel." Satan hated Israel because they were God's "Church," His chosen people, so he found a way to get them punished by inciting David to number them.

CHAPTER 6

It is a classic case from which we can learn much because Satan's methods of inciting those he wishes to destroy haven't changed. So, how did he incite David? A comprehensive understanding of human nature—including our own—makes it easy to figure it out. Notice that Satan didn't *force* David, he *incited* or *moved* him. That means that he *encouraged* or *motivated* him. David honestly thought that he was doing what "he" wanted to do. In fact, he was doing what Satan, his enemy, wanted him to do. David—like us—always had the freedom to *choose or change* his course. Satan's biggest weapon against us is always our pride and the lusts of our fleshly being, and he constantly uses them against us. He incites our emotions, feelings, and sensual desires to pursue what in reality does not exist.

Why would a man like David deliberately violate God's instruction not to number the people? Why would he refuse to take the counsel of his general in chief not to do it? Those are critically important questions, and they demand answers because there isn't one of us who is above being tempted in the same way. Why was it so important to David to know how many people he was king over? It was a desire born of **pride**. I'm sure that Satan planted the same kind of "sensible" ideas in David's mind that he plants in ours. "I can't see what harm there could possibly be in it." Besides, when I have to fight against other armies, it would be wise to know what my strength is." There is also the illusion of the power of being king over so many people.

Another fascinating passage is found in Job 1:6-12, "Now there was a day when the *sons of God* came to present themselves before the LORD, and Satan also came among them. The LORD said to Satan, 'From where do you come?' Then Satan answered the LORD and said, 'From roaming about on the earth and walking around on it.' The LORD said to Satan, 'Have you considered My servant Job? For there is no one like him on the earth, a blameless and upright man, fearing God and turning away from evil.' Then

Satan answered the LORD, 'Does Job fear God for nothing? Have You not made a hedge about him and his house and all that he has, on every side? You have blessed the work of his hands, and his possessions have increased in the land. But put forth Your hand now and touch all that he has; he will surely curse You to Your face.' Then the LORD said to Satan, 'Behold, all that he has is in your power, only do not put forth your hand on him.' So Satan departed from the presence of the LORD."

We learn that Satan is a "heavenly being" and that God allows him to come into His presence. We learn that the earth is now Satan's domain. We learn that he is aware of individuals, especially "good ones." We learn that his power is *limited*; he cannot touch Job unless God allows it, or he would have already done so. We learn that when God allows him to use it, he has tremendous power to inflict pain and to destroy. It is interesting to notice that apparently either he has *no power or desire* to heal or create; he can only destroy.

Mark tells us in 1:13, that when Jesus was in the wilderness forty days, He was *tempted by Satan*. We learn that Satan has the power to *tempt* even Jesus. We learn that he does not have power to *create* temptations; he only uses what *God has already created*.

In Mark 4:15, when Jesus tells the parable of the sower, He says concerning the seed sown on hard soil: "These are the ones who are beside the road where the word is sown; and when they hear, immediately *Satan* comes and *takes away the word* which has been sown in them." How does Satan take away the word? He does that by **diverting our attention**. He entices us with things that are not sinful or evil in appearance or in themselves: things like shopping, sports, work, Facebook, Twitter, and media games. Although individually they appear to be at best inane, trivial, inconsequential, and relatively harmless, the cumulative effect causes us to get so caught up in the here and now, in busyness, that there is no time to think about the message of the gospel and eternal consequences.

CHAPTER 6

Satan never tells us that the gospel is unimportant. He just tells us to get all of our financial, social, family, professional, and entertainment "ducks in a row" before we turn our attention to eternal matters. He knows that those things are so captivating, so "in our faces" that we will never get around to the other matters.

In Luke 13:16 Jesus says to the Pharisees concerning the woman that He had just healed on the Sabbath: "And this woman, a daughter of Abraham as she is, whom *Satan has bound* for eighteen long years, should she not have been released from this bond on the Sabbath day?" The passage seems to give credence to the idea that Satan was personally involved in this woman's disease. It may simply mean that Satan used her affliction to tempt her in some way, or it could mean that Satan actually imposed the affliction. Remember that he has the power to do so, but as in Job's case, *only* with God's permission. We are led to wonder if he still has that power and how many of our diseases are the result of Satan's "binding" with God's permission.

Luke 22:3 tells us that *"Satan entered* into Judas who was called Iscariot, belonging to the number of the twelve." We wonder how Satan "entered in" and does he still do that? He didn't force his way in, and he didn't overwhelm Judas. He simply used what already was in Judas: He was already a thief. He possessed a love of money, so Satan used the mental process that prompted Judas to *decide* to betray Jesus—*for money.*

The temptation was already there. Satan just used the 30 pieces of silver to further corrupt him. At the moment of his decision to act, Satan was in control of Judas, because Judas allowed *fleshly concerns* to dominate his decision. The warning for us is that Judas—just like us—was unaware of Satan's presence or influence. He thought he was doing the smart thing. Perhaps Satan "enters into" us at the moment when we decide to allow Satan to "tempt" us to do what we have already *thought about* doing. Remember, Satan has no power to "enter in" to anyone unless that person "allows" him.

In Luke 22:31 Jesus says to Peter: "Simon, Simon behold, Satan has demanded permission to sift you like wheat; but I have prayed for you, that your faith may not fail; and you, when once you have turned again, strengthen your brothers." It is comforting to note that Satan had to ask God for **permission** to "sift" Peter. It is *far less* comforting to realize that God *grants* Satan's request. This, "sifting like wheat," is most disturbing to us. I suspect that it has to do specifically with the temptation to deny Jesus. Whatever this "sifting" was, I know it must have been unpleasant. I wonder if Satan ever asks for the right to "sift" me. Looking back over my life, I am quite sure the answer is *yes*, and I am reminded of those times when his "sifting" accomplished his purposes.

I'm sure that it was comforting to Peter—I know that it is to me—that Jesus promised to pray for him. I believe that Jesus still prays for those whom Satan is allowed to "sift like wheat." He prays for us just as He prayed for Peter—not that we will not be "sifted." Sifting is necessary to spiritual growth. He prays that "our faith will not fail" and that after we have undergone this trial by fire, we will use the experience to strengthen our brothers and sisters.

In Acts 5:3 Luke says that Peter asked Ananias: "Why has Satan *filled your heart* to lie to the Holy Spirit and to keep back some of the price of the land?" This incident contains a critically important lesson from the Holy Spirit to every Christian. Satan can take what is initially a spiritual decision and turn it into a curse against the one who made the decision. The question is, "How did he do that?" By what *process* did Satan "fill their hearts"? Their hearts were not bad to begin with. We have no reason to believe that their original intentions were not noble and good.

How did Satan take such a noble decision and twist it to defeat these people? It was not by *supernatural intervention*. He did it by the power of "suggestion"—just as he did with Eve. "Why don't we just give part of the money and if everybody thinks we gave it all, we'll be praised, a lot of people are still benefited and nobody gets hurt."

One of the things we need to learn from this incident is how unaware Ananias is of the influence of Satan in the thought process that led him to lie. I'm sure that if we asked him why he lied, he would say that the desire for recognition was just too strong and besides, he couldn't see why it would possibly matter. After all, nobody got hurt. I'm sure that he would not have said, "The devil made me do it." It is critically important for us to think seriously about how "aware" or "unaware" we are of Satan's designs in our lives.

In Romans 16:20 Paul reassures the Christians at Rome with these words: "The God of peace will soon *crush Satan* under your feet. The grace of our Lord Jesus Christ be with you." Paul assures us that Satan's defeat is already determined; he cannot win, even in this world, unless **we allow him to**.

We read in 1 Corinthians 7:5: "Do not deprive each other, except perhaps by mutual consent and for a time, so that you may devote yourselves to prayer. Then come together again so that *Satan will not tempt you* because of your lack of self-control." Satan will use even good things to his purposes if we let him. Sexual intimacy is a good thing—a beautiful gift from God. Meditative prayer is a good thing, but to do either one to the neglect of the other will result in sin.

In 2 Corinthians 2:11, Paul speaks about the need for Christians to forgive those who have sinned against us: "…so that no advantage would be taken of us by Satan, for we are not ignorant of his schemes." Satan has a plan—a design, and it has to do with our condemnation. One of those designs is to use our pride to keep us from forgiving others. A failure to forgive is detrimental to both parties. Those who are unwilling to forgive condemn themselves to carry the burden of the wrong forever. They have no idea that they are serving Satan in so doing. The person who did the wrong carries the burden of the loss of the relationship and lives with the knowledge of his sin. Both parties live under the cloud of the wrong and bitterness and estrangement result. May God give each of us the spiritual discernment not to be ignorant of Satan's designs.

From 2 Corinthians 11:14: "Even *Satan disguises himself* as an angel of light." Satan does not approach those who struggle with sexual lust in the form of one who is aged, diseased, and ugly. He approaches in the form of youth, health, and beauty. He does not appeal to the liar in the form of a lost child, but in the form of a successful man of the world. He does not come to the greedy in the form of one who is starving and in rags, but as a financial consultant in a suit. He does not come to the righteous as a despotic dictator, but as a theologian.

The main lesson that we learn from Paul's instruction to put on our armor is that Christian warfare is fought at the *spiritual level*, and that war is perpetual. It may be less volatile one day and more volatile the next, but it never ends. Now we turn to the specific weapons God supplies to empower us to "stand firm" and to resist at the spiritual level.

Questions Over Ephesians 6:10-13

1. Where are Christian battles fought?
2. Who or what are the rulers, the powers, the world forces of this darkness and the spiritual [forces] of wickedness in the heavenly places?
3. Why is it important to know that?
4. Who is Satan and what is his origin?
5. What are his schemes and how does he go about accomplishing them?

CHAPTER 6

6. What is a "fallen angel?"
7. How do we know that there is a hierarchy of angels?
8. What is the angels' domain, and what is their "proper abode?"
9. How do we know when we are being "incited" by Satan?
10. What methods are available to us to resist Satan?
11. Why is Satan determined to bring Christians to destruction?
12. In the parable of the sower, how does Satan take away the word?
13. From the Luke 13:16 reference, does Satan still have power over disease?
14. How many of our diseases do you think are the result of Satan's "binding?"
15. How did Satan "fill Simon's heart?"
16. How did Satan "enter" Judas Iscariot?
17. What is Satan's favorite disguise?
18. Do Satan's schemes sometimes backfire on him?
19. How did Satan "block Paul's way?"
20. If we are fighting at the spiritual level, how do we defend ourselves and what weapons do we have with which to fight back?

[14] **"Stand firm therefore, having girded your loins with truth, and having put on the breastplate of righteousness."**
(Ephesians 6:14)

We are to surround ourselves with truth in the same way that a belt surrounds our bodies. In John 17:17 Jesus says in His high Priestly prayer; "Sanctify them in the truth; **Your word is truth.**" That means specifically that we are to surround ourselves with the Word of God—the Holy Scriptures. But there is another larger and more spiritual meaning as well, and that is that we are to surround ourselves with truthfulness. It is in this sense of truth that Jesus says in John 3:21: "But he who practices the truth comes to the Light, so his deeds may be manifested as having been wrought in God." Truth here is more encompassing than simply quoting Scripture; it has to do with the person of the Christ.

In John 8:31-32 John says to the Jews who had believed him, "If you continue in My word, then you are truly disciples of Mine; and you will know **the truth**, and **the truth** will make you free." There are two meanings to *truth* here. The first truth is that we are not disciples of the risen Christ simply because we *think* we are or because we *say* we are. We must inculcate the body of His teaching (the truth) to be His disciples. The second truth is that we must "know" (experience) the risen Christ in order to "know" the truth of His teaching. "Knowing" the risen Christ is a prerequisite to "knowing" the truth that He taught, and that is "the truth" that sets us free. What does it free us from? It frees us from everything that is not true.

This idea is born out in this passage from John 14:5-6: "Thomas said to him, 'Lord, we do not know where You are going, how do we know the way?' Jesus said to him, "**I am** the way, and **the truth**, and the life; no one comes to the Father but through me." A person may memorize the entire Bible and not "know" the truth, but a person cannot be a disciple of the risen Christ and not know the truth.

Regarding "the breastplate of righteousness," there is much to be understood about righteousness. I despair of being able to give a comprehensive overview of all that it means. First, the "breastplate" was not only designed to protect the wearer from harm; it was *emblematic* because it carried an insignia that declared *allegiance* to the person or country for which the one who wore it was fighting. I hope we can understand the significance of that. When people look at us, they are supposed to see our "insignia" and know who we serve.

CHAPTER 6

Scripture says much about *our* righteousness, God's righteousness, and *how* we become righteous. In Matthew 5:6, Jesus says: "Blessed are those who *hunger and thirst* for righteousness, for they shall be satisfied." Our righteousness *results* from an intense internal desire to be godly. Don't fail to notice the "Blessed are they." *Blessed* means that God looks with favor on those who hunger and thirst for righteousness and the promise is that He will satisfy them.

In Romans 1:17 Paul writes, "For in it (the gospel) the righteousness of God is revealed from faith to faith." God revealed His righteousness through *the gospel*, but it is **only revealed** to those who have *faith* in the gospel. The faith in the gospel that reveals God's righteousness leads to greater faith (*from* faith *to* faith). Romans 4:3 asks, "For what does the Scripture say? 'Abraham believed God, and it (his faith) was credited to him as righteousness.'" God counted the faith that Abraham had in His promises, as Abraham's righteousness.

Romans 3:21 says, "But now, *apart from the law*, the righteousness of God has been manifested, (in the gospel) being witnessed by the Law and the Prophets." Paul says that *now* (under God's new covenant), God has revealed His righteousness *apart from law*. Fulfilling His promise about the coming Messiah and His kingdom is the final demonstration of God's righteousness.

What does the Law reveal about God's righteousness? It reveals God's faithfulness to His promises and His covenant.

- "I will never again destroy the earth by water" (Genesis 9:11).
- "Seedtime and harvest shall not fail" (Genesis 8:22).
- "The steadfast love of the Lord never ceases" (Lamentations 3:22).
- "In your seed shall all the nations of the earth be *blessed*" (Genesis 22:18).

From Romans 4:9,11: "Is this *blessing* then on the circumcised, or on the uncircumcised also? For we say, "Faith was credited to Abraham as righteousness." 11: "and he received the sign of circumcision, a seal of the righteousness of the faith which he had *while uncircumcised*, so that he might be the father of all who believe *without being circumcised*, that righteousness might be credited to them."

Abraham was reckoned righteous *before* he was circumcised. Circumcision was God's *sign* that He had declared him righteous. His faith in God **was** his righteousness, not his works. His willingness to perform the act of circumcision was the *result* of his faith. Therefore his faith "was reckoned to him as righteousness" (Romans 4:22). Our righteousness results from our trust in God, not from our obedience or works. As noted above, although that trust may require that we perform many works, it is not the works themselves that are our righteousness; it is the "faith" that inspired us to perform them.

The discussion continues in Romans 9:30-32: "What shall we say then? That Gentiles, who did not pursue righteousness, attained righteousness, even *the righteousness which is by faith*; but Israel, pursuing a law of righteousness did not arrive at [that] law. Why? Because [they did] not [pursue it] by faith, but as though [it were] by works." Paul says that Gentiles succeeded in attaining righteousness because they pursued it on the *basis* of faith, but the Jews did not succeed in achieving righteousness, because they pursued it on the *basis* of works. The Jews could have achieved righteousness under the Law if they had pursued it on the basis of faith, as Abraham did. Striving for righteousness *based* on law or works is destined to fail. It simply cannot be done because that would establish a righteousness that is "apart from faith and the grace of God"—a righteousness based on what *we do* rather than on what *He does*.

There is a connection between works and righteousness.

CHAPTER 6

In Romans 6:16, Paul writes, "Do you not know that when you present yourselves to someone as slaves for obedience, you are slaves of the one whom you **obey**, either of sin, resulting in death, or of *obedience* resulting in *righteousness*?" Obedience is **not** righteousness; it **leads** to it. Our righteousness does not result from our efforts, but from our faith in God's efforts. However, faith that does not lead to obedience is meaningless and does not lead to righteousness because a failure to obey is the result of having no faith.

In Galatians 5:5, Paul writes, "For we through the Spirit, by faith, are waiting for the hope of righteousness." The righteousness that Paul speaks of here is Christ's final declaration to those who are at His right hand on judgment day: "Come you who are blessed of My Father, inherit the kingdom prepared for you from the foundation of the world" (Matthew 25:34). It is *by faith* in the Holy Spirit's indwelling that we have an "eager expectation" of heaven, where our righteousness will be perfected as the righteousness of God.

In 2 Timothy 2:22 Paul exhorts Timothy, "Flee the evil desires of youth and *pursue* righteousness, faith, love, and peace, along with those who call on the Lord from a pure heart" (NIV). Our righteousness must be "pursued." Although our righteousness is not the *result* of works, it is something for which we can and must **strive**. The difficult thing for us is that the idea of "pursuit" is immediately visualized as something physical—a "work." When we realize that "pursuing righteousness" is a *spiritual concept*, not a material one, we begin to understand why it must be pursued by "faith." Although a *physical response* may be necessary to achieve *spiritual goals*, those goals can never be achieved solely on the *basis* of a physical response.

See 2 Timothy 3:16: "All Scripture is inspired by God and profitable for teaching, for reproof, for correction, and for *training in righteousness*." The idea of being "trained in righteousness" is a fascinating one and must be incorporated into our concept of personal righteousness. The righteousness that we are "trained in" is God's righteousness not ours. The *knowledge of God* comes to us only through His revelation of Himself. Studying Scripture "trains us in righteousness" because it is only in Scripture that the righteousness of God is revealed.

Romans 10:3 explains yet another concept of righteousness: "For not knowing about God's righteousness, and seeking to establish their own, they did not subject themselves to the righteousness of God." The righteousness *that comes from God* is revealed to us in 2 Corinthians 5:21: "He made Him (Jesus) who knew no sin *to be sin* on our behalf, so that we might become the righteousness of God in Him." God's promise to Abraham, that in his seed all nations would be blessed, is fulfilled in all of those who **confess faith** in the risen Christ and are **born from above**.

This beautiful ***combination*** of the "*internal* confession of faith" accompanied by the *external* obedience of being baptized contains a microcosm of the entire scope of how the combination of faith and works results in the righteousness of God. When we are "born from above," God's forgives our sins, imparts the indwelling Holy Spirit, and we **become God's righteousness**. Notice that everything that "happens" in baptism is the work of God! It is critically important to remember that baptism is not a saving work. We don't **earn or deserve anything** because of it. Forgiveness of sin and receiving the Holy Spirit are based totally on the grace of God!

Questions Over Ephesians 6:14

1. What two truths are associated with surrounding ourselves with truth?
2. What two things was the breastplate designed to do?
3. What two things are required to be a disciple of the risen Christ?

CHAPTER 6

4. Why was God's righteousness revealed only to those who had faith?
5. How did God establish His righteousness apart from law?
6. What is the difference between striving for righteousness *based on* works and based on faith?
7. How do we wait for the hope of righteousness through the Holy Spirit?
8. What does the Law reveal about God's righteousness?
9. What does it mean to be "trained in righteousness?"
10. Why is striving for righteousness *based on* law or works destined to fail?
11. What is the hope of righteousness?
12. Discuss how the new birth combines perfectly the ideas of faith and works.
13. Discuss "everything that happens in baptism is the work of God."

[15] **"and having shod your feet with the preparation of the gospel of peace."**
(Ephesians 6:15)

An integral part of God's armor is what we wear on our feet. Notice that what we wear on our feet is not the "gospel of peace" itself, but the "readiness" that *comes from* the "gospel of peace." What is this "preparation"? It is the "study," the "prayer," the mental, spiritual, and emotional preparation in which Christians participate to be "ready" to share the good news with others at every opportunity. Peter puts it this way in 1 Peter 3:15: "But sanctify Christ as Lord in your hearts, always being ready to make a defense to everyone who asks you to give an account for the hope that is in you, yet with gentleness and reverence."

Why or what would cause a person to ask us about our hope?

I can tell you. It is because we act, speak, think, and conduct ourselves so **differently** from others, especially under difficult circumstances. If there is no "difference," there is no reason to ask!

The message we are to share is the gospel—the "Good News." But we need to look closely at why it is good news and *to whom* it is good news. John the Baptist preached "good news," but not everyone who heard John was happy about what they heard. In fact some were quite disgruntled and unhappy. Jesus preached "good news" and it got Him ridiculed, mocked, lied about, hated, and killed. Stephen preached "good news," and it got him stoned to death. Paul preached "good news," and it got him run out of town, beaten and thrown in jail. Phillip preached "good news" to the Eunuch, and he received it with joy. Peter preached "good news" on Pentecost and at the house of Cornelius and it forever changed their lives.

We must be prepared for a variety of conflicting reactions to our proclamation of the "good news." Why is the good news received so differently? One reason is that the "good news" *begins* with the "bad news." If you look closely at the examples I have given, you will easily discover that those who received the gospel as "good news" did so because they were *humble enough* to be convicted that they were lost in sin and under God's eternal condemnation. **Pride** caused others to reject the "good news." They simply were too **proud** to admit that they were sinners.

The "good news" is that we not only don't have to suffer the consequences of our sins here on earth, and ultimately, in the eternal fires of hell, but we can also live sin-free, guilt-free, positive, overcoming, and joyful lives here on earth—and live eternally with God when we die.

How do we "prepare" to proclaim the gospel? Our preparation begins with our own humble submission to the gospel message. The terrifying realization of what it means to be lost, accompanied by the incredibly exciting realization of being set free from the

CHAPTER 6

guilt of our sins—not just from the sins we have committed—but free from "sin itself," coupled with the hope of everlasting life with God, provides the daily spiritual impetus to share that message with others.

Why does Paul refer to the gospel as "the gospel of peace"? The peace that obedience to the gospel brings is first, peace between God and us. The result of Adam and Eve's sin was hostility between mankind and God; hostility between people; hostility between mankind and creation; and even hostility within each individual. Every action God has taken since the fall has been in an attempt to restore the peace that was lost there. The message of the cross is the final chapter in His attempt.

When we obey the gospel, peace is restored between us and God: "The Spirit himself testifies with our spirit that **we are children of God**" (Romans 8:16).

We have peace within ourselves:

- "Peace I leave with you; **My peace I give to you**; not as the world gives, do I give to you. *Let not your heart be troubled, nor let it be fearful*" (John 14:27).
- "These things I have spoken to you, that **in Me you may have peace**" (John 16:33).

There is peace among all of God's children: "And suddenly there appeared with the angel a multitude of the heavenly host praising God, and saying, 'Glory to God in the highest, And on earth **peace among men** with whom He is pleased'" (Luke 2:13-14).

The message of the cross sets in motion the "promise" of peace between God and His creation: "The creation waits in eager expectation for the children of God to be revealed. For the creation was subjected to frustration, not by its own choice, but by the will of the one who subjected it, in hope that **the creation itself will be liberated from its bondage to decay** and brought into the freedom and glory of the children of God" (Romans 8:19-21, NIV).

Questions Over Ephesians 6:15

1. What is the "preparation" that comes from the "gospel of peace?"
2. Elaborate on the *steps* we take to be "prepared" to share the good news?
3. Why is the gospel good news and to whom is it good news?
4. Why do you think that people respond to the gospel in such different ways?
5. What does it take to prepare us to proclaim the gospel?
6. Why does Paul refer to the gospel as "the gospel of peace?"
7. What four kinds of peace does the message of the cross bring?

16"In addition to all this, take up the shield of faith, with which you can extinguish all the flaming arrows of the evil one. (Ephesians 6:16)

Remember that all of these devices that we are to "put on, take up, wear, or carry" are designed to equip us for spiritual warfare. Although the shield, like the breastplate, was predominantly a protection device, it also usually carried an emblem that proclaimed allegiance. The classic *definition* of faith, one that has never been improved, comes from Hebrews 11:1: "Now faith is the assurance of things hoped for, the conviction of things not seen." The Bible says that faith **is** "conviction and assurance." But conviction and assurance are *feelings*, and that leaves no doubt about the "abstract nature" of faith. Faith is an "idea" that determines how we think, how we make decisions and how we act.

CHAPTER 6

Faith is supposed to equip us with the ability to "extinguish Satan's flaming missiles." We must remember that our faith is in Jesus, in God, in the Holy Spirit—not in our *understanding* of them—not in our experiences—not in the things that have happened to us or others—but in *them*. Our faith is that they *created* all things, *sustain* all things, and that all things in this world are under their control. Our faith is that they guide us, strengthen us, protect us, discipline us and love us.

What kinds of "flaming missiles" does Satan shoot at us? One that immediately comes to mind is the flaming arrow of doubt. Faith sustains us when we begin to doubt that living a Christian life is better—more joyful—than living a sinful one. Remember that sin is **desirable**. If it weren't, we wouldn't be so attracted to it. Faith sustains us when we begin to *doubt* that good is stronger than evil. Faith sustains us when we begin to think that sin "pays off" better than righteousness. Doubt causes us to ask with Job, "Why do the wicked prosper?" Faith assures us that we are living *the best possible life* as Christians. It is by faith that we see beyond this transient life and know that we don't have to get all of our living done in the narrow confines between our birth and death.

Other flaming missiles are those of materialism, disappointment, disillusionment, and discouragement. Faith helps us not only to accept the slings and arrows of outrageous fortune, but also to see in them the providential working of God. It is faith that leads us to see God *in all* of our circumstances. Our faith does not assure us that God will always bring us success, safety, and health, but it does assure us that He will act according to His purposes, mercy, wisdom, and our *eternal good.*

Faith in God's providence relieves us from the daily pressure of having to manage our minutes. It gives us a robust confidence in the power of goodness and tomorrow. Faith allows us to live with disappointment and disillusionment knowing that God is not particularly concerned with our earthly happiness. He is concerned that we are daily being molded into the likeness of His Son.

Satan also has in his quiver the flaming arrow of anxiety. Faith relives us from *anxiety*, especially those anxieties that are associated with things we cannot change. Jesus tells us in Matthew 6:25-34: "Therefore I tell you, **do not worry** (be anxious) about your life, what you will eat or drink; or about your body, what you will wear. Is not *life more than food*, and the body more than *clothes*? Look at the birds of the air; they do not sow nor reap or stow away in barns, and yet your heavenly Father feeds them. Are you not much more valuable than they? Can any one of you by worrying add a single hour to your life? And why do you *worry about clothes*? See how the flowers of the field grow. They do not labor or spin. Yet I tell you that not even Solomon in all his splendor was dressed like one of these. If that is how God clothes the grass of the field, which is here today and tomorrow is thrown into the fire, *will he not much more clothe you—you* **of little faith**? So **do not worry**, saying, 'What shall we eat?' or 'What shall we drink?' or 'What shall we wear?' For the pagans run after all these things, and your heavenly Father knows that you need them. But seek first His kingdom and his righteousness, and all these things will be given to you as well. Therefore **do not worry** about tomorrow, for tomorrow will worry about itself. Each day has enough trouble of its own" (NIV).

The sad truth is that this admonition has mostly fallen on deaf ears, even with Christians. In 60 years of ministry, counseling with and praying with physically, mentally, spiritually, and emotionally ill and troubled people, I have quoted this passage hundreds of times. It has been all too rare that it has had any noticeable positive impact. I confess that it has all too often had too little positive impact on me as well.

Faith allows us to be at peace with the "flaming missiles" of

CHAPTER 6

pain, heartache, and loneliness due to death, disease, or disaster and to look beyond them to what God's purposes are. Faith always asks what God is doing" because faith knows that "God works for good in **all circumstances** for those who love Him" (Romans 8:28). Faith gives us the confident patience to sing, "Faith is the victory that overcomes the world." Faith gives us the insight that teaches us that we do not see all ends and therefore God has purposes to accomplish in all of our circumstances.

Faith leads us to sing, "When all around my soul gives way, He then is all my hope and stay" ("My Hope Is Built," Mote/Bradbury, 1863). The incomprehensible mysteries of life are viewed with hope when seen through the eyes of faith. It is faith that leads us to obey the call of God, even when what He asks of us makes no sense, because as Oswald Chambers says, "Common sense is not faith, and faith is not common sense" (*My Utmost for His Highest*, 1924). Nothing that Jesus ever taught is common sense (turn the other cheek and tear your offensive eye out); it is "spiritual sense." It is faith that provides the motivation to take the next step—to get out of bed—to keep going—when we can see no reason to keep going.

Questions Over Ephesians 6:16

1. For what are all of these devices that we are to "put on" or carry designed to equip us?
2. The Bible *defines* faith as the assurance of things hoped for and the conviction of things we have not seen. What does that mean to you?
3. Of what does faith "assure" us?
4. What kinds of "flaming arrows" does Satan shoot at us? What kind has he shot at you in the past, and what kind is he shooting at you now? How has faith helped you to ward off those flaming arrows?

5. Why does Jesus tell us to "consider" (think about) the birds and the "flowers of the field?"

17a "Take the helmet of salvation," (Ephesians 6:17a)

In 1 Thessalonians 5:8 Paul says that we should, "be sober, having put on the breastplate of faith and love, and as a helmet, the *hope* of salvation." Hope and salvation are tied inseparably together. In Romans 5:4-5, Paul writes, "and endurance produces proven character, and proven character produces hope. This *hope will not disappoint us*, because God's love has been poured out in our hearts through the Holy Spirit who was given to us" (HCSB). Our hope of salvation never wavers, because God's love has been "poured out in our hearts by the Holy Spirit." John says in 1 John 4:19 that "We love because He first loved us." Sometimes it's hard to believe that He loves us, especially when our prayers are not answered as we hoped or expected, but through the "pouring out" work of the indwelling Holy Spirit, we are able, not only to *understand* the fullness of God's love, but also to actually *show* that love to others.

From Romans 8:24-25, "For in hope we have been saved, but hope that is seen is not hope; for who hopes for what he already sees? But if we hope for what we do not see, with perseverance we wait eagerly for it." What is it that we do not see? Paul tells us in Colossians 1:5 that it is our hope of heaven. Although John talks to us about heaven in the book of Revelation, almost all the words and images he uses to describe it begin with "like" as in; "The voice I heard was **like** the sound of many waters" (Revelation 14:2). John says, "The voice wasn't actually the sound of many waters, but that is as close as I can come." Finite human eyes and minds simply cannot grasp an infinite heaven or infinite love, but that causes us to live in **hope** of one day realizing its glory.

CHAPTER 6

Romans 15:13 contains three ideas about hope: "May the *God of hope* fill you with all joy and peace in believing, so that you will abound in hope **by the power of the Holy Spirit**." The first is that God is the source of our hope. We can only have hope because God has placed the capacity for it in our hearts and minds. The second is that the hope that God brings is also the source of the Christians' "joy." And the third is that we can "abound in hope" every day—in spite of negative circumstances—by the power supplied by the indwelling Holy Spirit.

Hebrews 6:19 teaches, "This hope we have as an **anchor of the soul**, a hope both sure and steadfast and one which enters within the veil." The Hebrew author tells us that our hope of salvation is sure, not "wishful thinking;" that it has substance because it is promised by God. Those promises are the "anchors" of our souls.

Paul, in 2 Corinthians 3:12, writes, "Therefore having such a hope, we use great boldness in our speech." Our hope leads to bold actions in proclaiming the gospel; in taking a bold stand against corruption, injustice, and immorality; in defending the poor; and in championing unpopular causes.

First Thessalonians 4:13 confirms, "But we do not want you to be uninformed, brethren, about those who are asleep (have died), so that you will not grieve as do the rest *who have no hope.*" Our hope of salvation brings confidence in the face of one of Satan's great flaming arrows—death. Confidence in the face of death is one of the most powerful testimonies to our faith that unbelievers can witness.

From Psalms 33:16-22: "The king is not saved by his great army; a warrior is not delivered by great strength. A horse is a false hope for victory; nor does it deliver anyone by its great strength. Behold, the eye of the LORD is on those who fear Him, on **those who hope** for His lovingkindness to deliver their soul from death and to keep them alive in famine. Our soul waits for the LORD; He is our help and our shield. For our heart rejoice in Him, because we trust in His holy name. Let Your lovingkindness, O LORD, be upon us, according as **we hope in You.**"

Questions Over Ephesians 6:17a

1. Name three things that hope does for us.
2. What is it that we do not see?
3. What is the relationship between the Holy Spirit and hope?
4. Name five things that hope leads us to do?
5. What does hope lead us to do in the face of death?

[17b] **"and the sword of the Spirit, which is the word of God." (Ephesians 6:17b)**

The final element in the armor of God is the only *potentially* "offensive" weapon we have, but the sword was also used defensively as well. Our sword is the sword of the Spirit—the Bible itself. In 2 Timothy 3:14-17, Paul admonishes, "You (Timothy), however, continue in the things you have learned and become convinced of, knowing from whom you have learned them, and that from childhood you have known the **sacred writings** which are able to **give the wisdom that leads to** salvation through faith in Christ Jesus. All Scripture *is inspired by God* and is *profitable* for *teaching,* for *reproof,* for *correction,* and for *training in righteousness*; so that the man of God may be adequate, equipped for every good work."

The Scriptures "instruct us for salvation" by revealing the way to live in a way that pleases God. They "instruct us" by equipping us to **reprove** and **correct those who stray from the truth.** They instruct us by "**training us** in righteousness;" they instruct us by providing what we need to be able to be involved in every good

CHAPTER 6

work. The Scriptures contain "**the** truth"—not "some truth," or "most truth," but "*the* truth!" As David writes in Psalms 119:160: "The sum of Your word is truth, and every one of Your righteous ordinances is everlasting." Jesus said of Himself, "I **am** the way, **the truth** and the life and no person can come to God, unless they come through me." The Scriptures are "the truth" in that they contain the revelation of Christ—the Messiah of God.

The following are some interesting and convicting passages from the Psalms:

- Psalm 19:7-12: "The law of the LORD is **perfect**, restoring the soul;

  The testimony of the LORD is **sure**, making wise the simple;

  The precepts of the LORD are **right**, rejoicing the heart;

  The commandment of the LORD is pure, enlightening the eyes;

  The fear of the LORD is clean, enduring forever;

  The judgments of the LORD are **true**; they are **righteous** altogether. They are more desirable than gold, yes, than much fine gold; sweeter also than honey and the drippings of the honeycomb. Moreover, by them Your servant is warned; in keeping them there is great reward. Who can discern his errors?"

- Psalm 119:9: "How can a young man keep his way pure? By keeping it according to Your word."

- Psalm 119:11: "Your word I have treasured in my heart, so that I may not sin against You."

- Psalm 119:81: "My soul languishes for Your salvation; I wait for Your word."

- Psalm 119:89: "Forever, O LORD, Your word is settled in heaven."

- Psalm 119:101: "I have restrained my feet from every evil way, that I may keep Your word."

- Psalm 119:105: "Your word is a lamp to my feet and a light to my path."
- Psalm 119:162: "I rejoice at Your word, as one who finds great spoil."
- Psalm 119:169: "Let my cry come before You, O LORD; give me understanding according to Your word."
- Psalm 138:2: "I will bow down toward Your holy temple and give thanks to Your name for Your lovingkindness and Your truth; for **You have magnified Your word according to all Your name**."

These are some closing references from the New Testament:

- John 17:17: "Sanctify them in the truth; Your word is truth."
- Acts 4:29: "And now, Lord, take note of their threats, and grant that Your bond-servants may speak Your word with all confidence."
- 2 Peter 1:20: "But know this first of all, that *no prophecy of Scripture* is a matter of one's own interpretation." Scripture is not a tool to be used to authorize personal agendas.
- Acts 17:11: "Now these were more noble-minded than those in Thessalonica, for they received the word with great eagerness, *examining the Scriptures* daily to see whether these things were so."

All of our ideas about God, the Church, salvation, morality, marriage, love, raising children, and life itself must be based on Scripture. The Bible is the final voice of authority in *all things*; it is the standard by which we live. When Jesus was tempted by Satan, He deferred to Scripture for His defense. He answered all of Satan's attempts by saying "It is written." The Bible is not a book of questions with no answers; it is a book of answers to all of our questions.

CHAPTER 6

A special relationship exists between the "author"—the Holy Spirit—and His manuscript—the Scriptures. That is why the Bible is referred to as, "The Sword of the Spirit." When we say that the Bible is "inspired," we are saying is that it is "Spirit-breathed." In practical terms, that means that the Holy Spirit motivated, instructed, and guided those who actually did the physical writing. By "motivating" I mean that He "prompted" or "incited" the men who wrote to write. "The word of the Lord came to Jonah, the son of Amittai saying, 'Arise, go to Nineveh that great city and cry out against it....'" (Jonah 1:1, NIV).

How did the word of the Lord come to Jonah? Peter tells us in 2 Peter 1:21: "No prophecy was ever made by an **act of human will**, but men **moved by** the Holy Spirit spoke from God."

The Holy Spirit not only "inspired" the writing of the Bible, He "uses" it to do His *convicting work*. The exact process by which the Holy Spirit uses Scripture, along with His own "outpoured" personal influence on those who proclaim the gospel and those who hear it, to convict people of sin and of righteousness remains a mystery to us, but we know that He does that because Jesus said that He would (John 7:37-39). Why two people can hear the same message and react in a totally differently is difficult to understand.

Questions Over Ephesians 6:17b

1. What are the "offensive" qualities of the Bible—the "sword of the Spirit?"
2. Discuss the following statement: "All of our ideas about God, the Church, salvation, morality, marriage, love, raising children, and life itself must be based on Scripture."
3. Why are the Scriptures called "The Sword of the Spirit?"
4. What is the difference between the "guiding" and the "instructing" work of the Spirit?

5. What special relationship exists between Scripture and the Holy Spirit?
6. What do you think causes two people to hear the same message and react in a totally differently way?

¹⁸ "With all prayer and petition pray at all times in the Spirit, and with this in view, be on the alert with all perseverance and petition for all the saints, ¹⁹and [pray] on my behalf, that utterance may be given to me in the opening of my mouth, to make known with boldness the mystery of the gospel, ²⁰ for which I am an ambassador in chains; that in [proclaiming] it I may speak boldly, as I ought to speak."
(Ephesians 6:18-20)

What does it mean to "pray in the Spirit"? It seems a strange thing to me that in my 77 years of church attendance, my 70-plus years of Bible study, my 60 years of preaching and attending Christian colleges, I have no recollection of ever hearing a sermon on this verse, (outside of my own) or heard it discussed in a class. I have seldom heard it referred to or even acknowledged. I suppose that that means that we are uncomfortable with what it seems to say and would have preferred that it had never been said.

Briefly, I would suggest two things that I believe it means. (For a much more complete discussion please see my book, *A Restoration View of The Holy Spirit*, or order my CD set on this topic.) It means to pray with an awareness of the Spirit and His *intercessory involvement* in our prayers. Romans 8:26-27 teaches: "In the same way the Spirit also helps us in our weakness; for we do not know how to pray as we should, but *the Spirit Himself intercedes* for us with groanings too deep for words; And He, who searches the heart knows what is the mind of the Spirit is because He *intercedes* for the saints according to the will of God."

CHAPTER 6

What that means is that when I pray, the Holy Spirit arranges, rearranges, edits, and turns my finite human words into infinite spiritual thoughts and presents them before the throne of God. The Holy Spirit says to the Father, "Here is what John **means**." Another part of this idea is that because the Spirit *indwells* us, He *understands* the emotions, longings, griefs, heartaches, gratitude, and joys that lie so deeply within us that we cannot place them into words. He then translates them into spiritual emotions and says, "Here is what John **feels**."

Another way we can pray in the Spirit is to pray with a *consciousness* of the indwelling Spirit and the leading and guiding He does. Remember the passage from Ephesians 5:19 about being *filled with the Spirit* "**as** you sing psalms, hymns, and spiritual songs." In the same sense that we can be filled with the Spirit **as we sing**, we can be filled with the Spirit **as we pray**.

Paul exhorts the Ephesian congregation to pray for the Church in general; to pray for him personally; to pray *specifically* that he might *receive a message from God* and that he might preach that message boldly. The only way God can answer that prayer is through the indwelling Spirit.

Questions Over Ephesians 6:18-20

1. What does it mean to "pray in the Spirit?"
2. Would you say that you had ever done that? If your answer is *no*, why do you think that is?
3. In all of our emphasis on prayer, why do you think that we have so little to say about this passage?
4. What does Paul mean when he says that: "*the Spirit intercedes* for the saints according to the will of God?"
5. What does the Spirit actually do in His intercessory work?

²¹ But that you also may know about my circumstances, how I am doing, Tychicus, the beloved brother and faithful minister in the Lord, will make everything known to you. ²² I have sent him to you for this very purpose, so that you may know about us, and that he may comfort your hearts. ²³ Peace be to the brethren, and love with faith, from God the Father and the Lord Jesus Christ. ²⁴ Grace be with all those who love our Lord Jesus Christ with incorruptible love."
(Ephesians 6:21-24)

Apparently, Tychicus is going to physically carry this letter to the congregation in Ephesus. Paul is relying on him to tell them all of the details of his present circumstances. My comments on this closing passage are contained in the introduction to the book.

His closing benediction is a prayer for God to bring peace, love, grace, and faith to them. I suppose it is natural for us to skim over the benediction with little or no comment, because it seems rather superfluous—just the proper and accepted way to conclude a letter between Christians. I only want to say that I don't believe that is what either Paul or the Holy Spirit intended. I don't think that they said, "Well, we have to have an appropriate ending, so let's say something nice, comforting and appropriate. I believe that Paul took his prayer seriously and expected his audience to do so, too.

www.ingramcontent.com/pod-product-compliance
Lightning Source LLC
Chambersburg PA
CBHW060516100426
42743CB00009B/1337